CARLA'

To Jake
Solidarity!
Ken Loach

CARLA'S SONG
Paul Laverty

faber and faber
LONDON · BOSTON

First published in 1997
by Faber and Faber Limited
3 Queen Square London WCIN 3AU

Photoset by Parker Typesetting Service, Leicester
Printed in England by Clays Ltd, St Ives plc

Paul Laverty is hereby identified as author of this work in accordance with
Section 77 of the Copyright, Designs and Patents Act 1988

A CIP record for this book
is available from the British Library
ISBN 0–571–19162–2

2 4 6 8 10 9 7 5 3 1

CONTENTS

Paul Laverty

Ken Loach

The thing that I saw on your face
No power can disinherit:
No bomb that ever burst
Shatters the crystal spirit.

George Orwell

INTRODUCTION

I remember getting on a plane in Glasgow with a hangover, bent double with a bag of medical books for delivery to a Scottish doctor – those thick, shiny, indestructible type of books – changing planes in London, changing in Leningrad, changing in Moscow, changing in Ireland (couldn't board there), changing in Cuba, arriving in Nicaragua, waiting five hours for a bus, scrambling on like a lunatic, stuffed in tighter than a fat sardine, arriving in Esteli in the north of the country four hours later, and looking for an address using non-existent Spanish. Dehydrated and totally disorientated, I'll never forget this wee round woman called Esperanza dishing me out an enormous plate of tripe soup, which I couldn't refuse. As I tried to chew, chasing this big bastard of a lump of tripe, which seemed to expand by the minute, around my mouth, all I could think was, 'What the hell am I doing here?'

Over the next six months (from October 1984 to March 1985) before returning to Scotland, I crossed paths with many other travellers: ex-CIA, ex-Vietnam vets, transcendentalists meditating for peace, adventurers, would-be heroes, you name it . . . even a bald bishop with an expensive wig, liberation theologians from São Paolo, human rights workers from Manila, plumbers from Germany, peace activists from the States, and holiday-makers who could live like kings for a few dollars changed on the black market. Yet the most frequent visitors to Nicaragua in the eighties were the tens of thousands of ordinary people, organized in their different types of solidarity groups round the world, who, for whatever reason, were somehow touched by the Nicaraguan Revolution, and were determined to support it.

My own interest in Nicaragua was crystallized after watching a documentary presented by a Jesuit priest, Padre Gorostiaga. Several things struck me. First of all, this young revolutionary society organized a massive literacy crusade and taught its people to read and write. They just did it. Sheer bloody-minded determination. Literacy, they insisted, was the premise to a democratic culture. Even the UN organization UNESCO was amazed and said the Nicaraguan experience should be used as a model for the rest of Latin America. It was a similar story with health. They wiped out polio and considerably reduced other diseases to applause from the World Health Organization. Yet, the programme claimed, these very same doctors, nurses and teachers were being tortured and murdered by the Contras, who were in turn organized, financed and trained by the United States Government.

It's almost hard to believe now; but, in the words of the US State Department, Nicaragua, this tiny little country with a population not much more than the Strathclyde region, was the second most important foreign policy priority for the US in the eighties; the first being its relationship with the Soviet Union. Why was it so dangerous? Why did the US government spend billions of dollars, in the words of Ronald Reagan, to make Nicaragua 'cry uncle', i.e. surrender?

A year later, in February 1986, and with a bit more Spanish (this time they had dumped a monster-sized accordion on us for delivery to a theatre group), I returned to Nicaragua with Kate Hughes, a Scottish midwife, and Richard Watson, a doctor. We were supported by a solidarity organization called Scottish Medical Air to Nicaragua (SMAN), which ran with amazing stamina for a long time from Des Tierney's and Gillian Brear's flat in Glasgow. SMAN sent medical personnel to Nicaragua and was building a health centre, but its main focus was work back home, trying to mobilize public opposition to Thatcher's support for Reagan in Central America.

My colleagues in Nicaragua, Margaret Craig, Fiona Crawford, Mike Bonnar, Nick Lockhart, Richard and Kate, all worked in health. I had previously worked as a lawyer in Glasgow and, to cut a long story short, I ended up working for a domestic Nicaraguan human rights organization, which did its best to monitor human rights abuse in the war zones.

What I saw and heard over the next two and a half years formed the raw material for *Carla's Song*. What stunned me from the very beginning was the creativity, intelligence and imagination behind the violence. It was systematic, well-funded and unrelenting.

There was, of course, the obvious military stuff. The Contras, with USA intelligence support and satellite photos, would carry out ambushes against civilians and the army, blow up strategic targets like the port of Corinto, bridges, pylons and co-operatives. But much more insidious was the 'invisible muscle': the economic embargo had a devastating effect on the economy; the diplomatic pressure against third countries not to supply oil or other key materials; the cutting off of loans via the IMF and the World Bank; and a host of other diplomatic offensives. All this had the effect of grinding Nicaragua down (this is why there was always a massive battle to get on a ramshackle bus) and, of critical importance, it meant that more of the country's meagre resources would be diverted away from civilian use to the war.

Sometimes you could just sit there and observe the terrible symmetry of it all, meticulously clicking together. Contra troops would co-ordinate attacks at the same time as the US Navy completed manoeuvres off the coast, both coinciding with statements from the US State Department or even with Reagan meeting Contra leaders, primed of course with wonderfully prepared soundbites and images eagerly swallowed up by the majority of the international press. Reagan shook their hands, beamed at the cameras, and called the Contra leaders 'the moral equivalent of our founding fathers'. So many talented, educated people were behind this sham, dressed in suits, going back to their families, all playing their part in systematically tearing a country apart. The scale and 'style' of it, wrapped up in the language of freedom, still amazes me.

Meanwhile, through my work, I began to find out in detail what was happening in the countryside, either from travelling to communities attacked by the Contras, or via reports from people living there. The cruelty was beyond the imagination. Part of my work was to present information to the dozens of foreign delegations who arrived there on fact-finding missions. It is extremely difficult to talk about carnage. In some way the mind doesn't connect; it's too disturbing. The fact that it is premeditated and systematic is even more difficult to accept, especially for so many North American delegations who realized for the first time where their tax dollars were going.

Hundreds of memories come to mind, but one sticks. We got a

report one night of a Contra attack on a co-operative. There was the usual chaos and mayhem. A young woman was shot and injured and couldn't run. Her parents somehow got away to the safety of a trench, only to hear the Contras in the near distance torturing their daughter whose voice they recognized. They found her dead the next day with her breasts cut off.

On another day I interviewed a young Contra, barely twenty, who had been captured by the Sandinistas. He had been with the Contras for several years and had an array of minor bullet scars as testimony to many encounters. He told me he had been involved in dozens of ambushes. While staring out of the window he drifted off into a disturbed reverie and, with an imaginary knife in his hand, he swished it back and forth, describing in detail how he finished off those lying wounded after they had ambushed a vehicle.

I got a sense of the incredible human hurt behind each statistic, of the complexity and trauma behind each life that would never be the same whether they were victim or even Contra perpetrator. I'll never forget a skinny ten-year-old kid, shaking in uncontrollable sobs, miserable to the core, howling beside his dead uncle, or a father in hushed calm tones talking about his kidnapped son. As we talked to delegates and had our reports printed, I had a profound sense we were still pissing in the wind against this huge blanket of misinformation that crushed everything in its path and could successfully dictate the agenda as if it were indeed a fight for freedom and human rights against the 'totalitarian Communist regime' of the Sandinistas.

I suppose that was the reason why I wanted to see if we could make a film. I wanted to see if we could take just one character, and give human shape to just one of these thousands of statistics, by telling his or her story, set against the real backdrop of Nicaragua.

CARLA'S SONG

I returned to Scotland with this idea firmly in mind, but without a clue about how to go about it. But I did receive fantastic encouragement and help from many people.

I prepared some character profiles and a storyline and then bombarded the film world, who in turn bombarded their wastepaper bins with my storyline. I, in turn, bombarded my big bin with their rejection letters, when I was lucky enough to get an answer. 'Quite unrealistic' appeared again and again with all the gravitas and certainty of a papal encyclical.

Then I wrote to Ken Loach and he phoned me up. From the outset, Ken was incredibly curious. We just had a right good chat. Never once did he ask me if I had ever written a script. He was just full of straightforward questions.

I met up with Ken again on several occasions and also with Sally Hibbin, who produced many of Ken's films. We talked and discussed different approaches. We prepared another outline and I got a commission from the Scottish Film Production Fund to write a script.

The first draft of the screenplay seemed to pop out and then the fun started. Over the next three years, in between Ken's other projects that were more advanced (*Raining Stones, Ladybird, Ladybird* and *Land and Freedom*) we met up to collaborate on the script. The process is something live and full of possibility, right to the end. We made lots of changes after each preparatory trip to Nicaragua, after we knew who the actors were and sometimes even the night before a scene was shot. Changes were also made spontaneously by the actors during the performance.

Nicaragua is not an easy place in which to make a film and there were many exploratory visits. It was crucial to get the co-operation of the new government and, of course, the army – quite apart from the usual challenge of finding the locations and actors. On our first trip we had a fantastic piece of luck in meeting up with Frank Pineda, a Nicaraguan cameraman, who had filmed much of the war, and his wife Florence Jaugey, who had directed and edited her own films and documentaries. Between them they had a firm idea of what was possible and knew Nicaragua like the back of their hands. They quickly grasped how Ken and Sally had worked on previous films, and how keen we were to co-operate and work with Nicaraguan grass-root organizations. They helped us through.

They were also vital in helping us find Carla. First of all, it was important for us that she should be Nicaraguan – that sounds manifestly obvious, but it's not at all obvious in the film world. For the story she had to be able to speak some English; to be able to really play the part she had to understand what the revolution was about.

There are very few actors in Nicaragua, but many musicians and dancers. We had several casting sessions in Nicaragua (including one hectic day of open casting advertised on radio and TV; three men phoned up offering to come in drag), one in Los Angeles and one in Miami. The vast majority of those who spoke English had little idea of what had happened in the revolution. Those who had lived through it one way or another, for example working in the countryside with the literacy brigades, had never had the opportunity to learn English.

We found several strong candidates, including Oyanka Cabezas, a dancer. She was terrific in the acting improvisations Ken set for her. The only problem was, she did not speak a word of English. We invited her to come over to England and she got stuck into a crash-course in English.

Ken had worked with Bobby Carlyle before in *Riff-Raff*, and in the improvisations between them it was not difficult to imagine the characters of George and Carla.

The time, talent and tidy minds needed to get actors to turn up on a certain day at a certain time and then film it all, never ceases to amaze me. I saw it all, but I'm still not sure how they did it. The fact that half of it was shot in Glasgow in December (the day we left the Clyde completely froze over) and the other half in Nicaragua at the end of the rainy season, just made it all the more difficult. Ken's habit of shooting a film in continuity makes it more complicated for logistics and finance, but much better for the actors. So the flashback scenes were shot first in Nicaragua to allow Oyanka to carry those experiences in her head. We then flew back to Scotland to shoot the first half of the film and then back again to Nicaragua to do the second half.

RETURNING TO NICARAGUA

I arrived in Nicaragua for the first time in October of 1984, just before Nicaragua's first free elections in which the Sandinistas won 67 per cent of the vote. I emphasize this because these are the great invisible elections. They were monitored by international observers at the time, but seem to have been wiped from the collective memory of commentators, journalists and producers.

The fact that the Sandinistas won a popular mandate made no difference to the US funding of the Contra war. The fact that the United States were regularly condemned by the General Assembly of the United Nations made no difference. And, in a spectacular snub to the civilized world, on the same day that the World Court at The Hague found the US guilty of nine different violations of international law, the US Congress awarded another $100 million to the Contras.

In 1990, according to the media, Nicaragua had its first 'really, really' free elections. George Bush had now replaced Ronald Reagan, and to help the Nicaraguans exercise their free vote for which candidate took their fancy, he made it clear that if they, in all their wisdom, again voted for the Sandinistas, the US would continue to fund the war and continue with the economic embargo. If, on the other hand, they should vote for Violeta Chamorro, a figurehead for fourteen opposition parties moulded together by the US, the Nicaraguans would find the US in favour of peace, promising a mini-Marshall plan.

Diligently, the world's media descended on Nicaragua for the election day, diligently monitoring the polling booths, diligently checking voter lists, diligently witnessing lines of Nicaraguans queuing to vote and diligently reporting the result of Nicaragua's 'really, really' first free elections. Violeta Chamorro replaced Daniel Ortega as the new President of Nicaragua.

In the few months following the elections up to the change of government, senior Sandinista figures managed to destroy what ten years of war and continuous propaganda had not been able to do: they lost their moral capital in the eyes of many Nicaraguans who had been their supporters because a certain section of these figures were seen to gain personally – whether in terms of property or money in a pre-government hand-over 'hand-out', called the *pinata*.

We started the Nicaraguan part of *Carla's Song* in January 1996 after six years of 'peace'. A very visible war, one of troops, guns and uniforms (and compulsory military service, which deeply damaged Sandinista popularity) had disappeared.

But a more insidious war permeated life. At every set of traffic lights in Managua, young children, some taking care of babies, were begging at traffic lights. Young glue-sniffers wandered around abandoned buildings. Outside bars, children as young as twelve were selling their bodies. Today, Nicaragua, as a percentage of its GNP, has the highest repayments on its foreign debt in history. This means that every man and woman, every child at those traffic lights, per capita, owes $2,600 in international debt; all this in a country where annual earnings average $250. It doesn't take a bookie to figure out that this debt, and its ever cumulative interest, is unpayable. Unrelenting misery confronts Nicaraguans, destroying any possibility of ever starting from scratch. It is nothing other than macro-economic torture. The banking memoranda and jargon of 'extended structural adjustment facilities' of the IMF disguise the gutter morality of the back-street money lender. At least the latter has no pretension.

When I was doing a video diary for the BBC, I spoke to those kids at the traffic lights. They all had malnourished, pinched little faces streaked with sweat and car emissions, but all jumped around madly in front of the camera, as you would expect. One little girl I remember very distinctly because she had a burnt hand. I asked her what she wanted to say to people outside Nicaragua. She stopped jumping about and stood deadly serious: 'I would like enough money to eat and go to school, so I don't have to be here every day begging at traffic lights.'

I remembered my first visit to Esteli in the north of the country in 1984. A local government official spoke to a foreign delegation and asked them not to give money to beggars: 'We take pride in looking after our own people.' Changed times.

But there were other days in the shoot that would really give you heart. This is an entry from a rough diary of 11 January 1996:

Day 28 of shoot – Pan-American highway, by La Trinidad, Nicaragua.
A huge voice boomed from a tiny kid; his father accompanied him on a guitar and then some started dancing. The rest formed a circle and clapped and celebrated around the dancers. The delight and excitement was infectious. I burst out laughing and started dancing too; still not even 6 a.m.

I had met these *campesinos* (farm workers) earlier in the week at their co-operative, just north of Esteli. Forty families now had what once belonged to one Somocista landlord who had fled at the time of the revolution in 1979. Young and old, men and women, were bringing in sugar cane on oxen carts, boiling it over a huge cauldron and making sweets. 'We're not rich, but we won't starve.'

Lucinda Broadbent, with whom I worked in Nicaragua, was co-ordinating the casting with Ken. She told me they had even composed a song 'to welcome the film'. After the dancing finished I asked one of the older men how he felt. 'Ready, willing and happy to tell you a little about our lives.' And that's what they did in Scene 48, 'the bottle of whisky scene'. It's very short, simple and takes place on a bus. Five *campesinos* on top (the rest inside) joke with Carla and George. But as the scene develops, what they reveal of their lives, in reality so touched Oyanka, which in turn so touched Bobby Carlyle, that all this touched the crew as they filmed. When they came home that night everyone was strangely quiet.

The rushes came through on video a week later. I tried to figure out what got to me, though I had no idea whether it would touch an audience in the same way. Their simple elegance, the honesty of Oyanka's emotional response, and her clumsy translation for Bobby, was way beyond anything I could ever have written. It was caught, first of all, by having *campesinos* who had suffered under the Somoza dictatorship and whose lives had been changed by the revolution involved in this scene, by Ken's instinct in casting Oyanka who cared and understood what the lives of *campesinos* were all about, by Bobby's openness to Oyanka, and by the skill of a really sensitive team who captured the unexpected: the beauty of collaboration. And how they loved that bottle of Glenmorangie.

Some of the older *campesinos* explained how they had been treated like slaves. In gentle tones, but with a fierce determination, they emphasized that the land would never be handed back to the Somocista landlord. One added: 'The revolution taught me to read. You can't rub that out.' This particular co-operative had been functioning successfully since 1979, but other co-operatives have folded because they were unable to get credit to buy seed and other implements.

Throughout the shoot we kept bumping into more and more people with incredible stories. Ken always talks about the abundance of stories you find, more than can ever be used, but you just hope the ones you do use will somehow do justice to the bigger picture.

One day we were shooting in Managua when some of the men hanging around in the street introduced me to 'Commandante Hueso' (Commander Bone), his nickname because he was so lanky and skinny. Hueso had a nervous tic in one eye, caused by the remnant of a bullet in his head, which was too dangerous to remove. He had gained some notoriety as a teenager by organizing ambushes against Somoza's National Guard before the revolution. He had fought against the Guard in the final insurrection, and after that he had gone into the mountains to fight for years against the Contras. Here he was now, standing on a street corner with dozens of other men, desperate for work, desperate to do something useful. There was this terrible bewilderment on his face; he wanted action, he wanted to fight the enemy, but somehow the enemy had disappeared in front of his eyes. He wandered around like one lost soul in a sea of 70 per cent unemployment. He reminded me of Tom Joad in *The Grapes of Wrath*, desperately trying to understand who or what was making the decisions that set the parameters of his totally frustrated life.

Another day we were doing a tiny little scene where two women stop at a cross to say a prayer at the scene of an ambush. It would last no more than fifteen seconds on film. I spoke to the women later. Both had lost their sons. One of them, in very gentle tones, and without any tears, told me, 'My son was burned alive. I never ever want to see war again. I don't want this for our children, but it is really really important that people understand what happened to us.' I was touched that they felt so strongly about participating in the film.

The shoot ground on and I suppose this unfussy, committed team, who were such a laugh to be with, got it done by the skin of their teeth. (Martin Johnson, Designer, has worked with Ken for over twenty-five years. Barry Ackroyd, Director of Photography, and Ray Beckett, Sound, and many others, have worked with Ken on all of his recent films.) The heat, the poor infrastructure (you can't just dial up *campesinos* who live in the middle of the countryside to change plans) and a hundred and one unforeseen complications, plus the language problem, made this an incredibly difficult shoot for everyone concerned. Towards the end, many of them got sick, including Bobby who missed a day's filming for the first time in his life. Ken, too, got whacked on the last two days but somehow got through it by sheer willpower. For the first time I had seen this man who never stops really exhausted. Now I see why all those other film companies wrote back saying it was 'quite unrealistic' to shoot a film in Nicaragua. Unrealistic, but somehow possible.

BRINGING THE FILM BACK TO NICARAGUA

Eight and a half rolls of celluloid is enough to give you a hernia. I nearly missed the plane in Madrid and therefore had to bring the film print on as hand luggage. Here it was, *Carla's Song*, ready for showing after months and months of editing, composing the music, doing the subtitles and lots of other things I still don't understand. But there it was, October 1996, in a big, heavy, cardboard box.

Ken and Sally promised the Nicaraguans we worked with that we would bring the film back once it was finished. I think they wanted to believe us, but didn't quite. The little experience they had with other film companies had convinced them otherwise.

We arrived at a very tense time, just three weeks before the elections in which Daniel Ortega, of the Sandinistas and Arnoldo Aleman, of the right-wing Liberal Alliance, were running within a few percentage points of each other.

The Sandinistas were more concerned about the content of the film than anyone. They had just signed an accord with ex-Contra leaders promising them major government portfolios if they won. Meanwhile, Aleman, backed by Cubans and Nicaraguans with money in Miami, ran a well-financed campaign, blaming the Sandinistas for the war: full-page adverts of Ortega superimposed on images of funerals from the eighties.

It's quite surreal to see history rewritten before your eyes quite so crudely. It didn't matter that William Casey, Reagan's campaign manager and then head of the CIA, got in contact with President Galtieri of Argentina and sent the thugs apprenticed in the dirty war (in which thousands went missing) to Honduras to train the remnants of Somoza's National Guard and turn them into the Nicaraguan Contras. It didn't matter that the CIA financed them, trained them, and instructed them. Despite the US's creation of the Contras and the billion-dollar investment in attacking Nicaragua, the Sandinistas still somehow caused the war.

It was like some strange double twist on reality. The Sandinista leadership did their very best not to talk about the war, while the right wing were appealing to the voters to 'remember the past'. Then we arrived with a film set almost ten years ago in the middle of the war.

As we drove in with the film to one of the very few functioning cinemas in Managua, we passed the same little girl with the burnt hand begging at the same traffic lights. January to October. Still there.

THE SCREENINGS

I don't know what Machiavelli looked like, but since these screenings in Managua I've been a firm believer in reincarnation. The man who ran the Cinemateca cinema gave us a right royal run around. Just before the very first screening for cast and crew, a part from the projector, which had worked perfectly the previous evening, mysteriously had to be repaired at some unspecified workshop. (He promised to show the film for a two-week run which, of course, he never did. The last report we got from Nicaragua was that he still hadn't shown the film but was showing Somocista propaganda footage to the supporters of the new President, Aleman.) Once again Frank Pineda and Florence Jaugey saved our bacon. They had somehow or other got their hands on two old Soviet projectors that were used in the eighties to bring film to countryside locations. At short notice we set them up in the cinema and ran the film. They made as much noise as a steelworks on a quiet day, and for the whole first half the subtitles shook so badly it was virtually impossible to read them. Suddenly, halfway through the film, Machiavelli appeared with the missing part which had mysteriously rectified itself.

In the evening we had a press screening. With half an hour to go there was such a fierce storm that the main electricity plant blew up, knocking out power for the central part of the city. The press conference continued afterwards in total darkness, and without the journalists knowing how the film ended. We read next day that six people had drowned in Managua.

The following day we brought the film up to the main university in Managua and showed it with just a few hours' notice. Almost 300 students squeezed into a small hall as the old projectors rattled out the images on a scabby old wall. It didn't matter. I didn't quite realize what a unique experience it was for them to see and hear Nicaraguans, just like them, on screen. There was a fantastic debate afterwards about what the war meant, the reasons for it, whether it was an East–West or North–South conflict, what the revolution tried to achieve and, most of all, what it was like for students of a previous generation to live through the war. Several of the older students who had experienced it were very emotional and ended up in tears.

We brought the film up to the north of the country to the little town of Ducuale, where we had actually filmed. There was no such thing as a cinema and I doubt all but a handful of its people had ever been to a cinema. The plan was to show it in the main square. Our hearts fell as we approached the mountains and saw an almighty storm in the distance. It was still raining when we arrived, but it was just magic to meet up with old friends again who had acted in *Carla's Song* and built the houses that were eventually blown up in the film.

We couldn't believe our luck as the skies cleared and we caught sight of the stars. Everyone sprang into action. Technicians connected up wires to the cables overhead, a massive painted screen was unrolled up front and suddenly bodies with chairs and benches started appearing from everywhere as the houses emptied. Dozens and dozens of kids ducked down at the front. Cows walked past, pigs rustled, dogs barked and chickens picked between the bodies as the old projectors sprang into life.

Many of the villagers were not able to read, or at least read fast enough for the subtitles in the Glasgow part of the film. So Salvador, one of the actors in the film, performed heroics as he clung to an old microphone from which he got periodic shocks as he gave a running commentary for the villagers with all the timing and humour of a stand-up comic.

In among all this I can still see the grisly-bearded silhouette of an old *campesino*, sitting crouched down among the children, watching in total and absolute concentration the dancing images just twelve feet from him as if it were all some kind of magic. Just before George and Carla, in the film, drove into the very square in which they were all seated, the rain started. Nobody moved, bar a mother with a child at her breast. George and Carla's jeep sped into the little town of Ducuale. The children squealed in recognition. I caught sight of Ken away back in the distance with just a hint of a smile.

The following day we showed the film in Esteli, one of the main northern towns which had risen up three times against Somoza (and paid a bloody price) before he finally fled. It was at the forefront of the war during the eighties. It has a huge barn of a cinema for 800 people, which had been lying empty for years. Over a thousand people squeezed in before the organizers managed to get the gates shut to prevent it becoming any more dangerous. A crowd built up outside and totally ignored and insulted the few desperate policemen who tried to maintain order, shouting for the gates to be opened again. Inside, all the corridors were chock-a-block. A dog ran among legs, along with lots of young boys up to mischief in the madness. As the trusty projectors sprang into action again I could see the silhouette of bicycles, babies and assorted food stalls on screen as people tried to make their way down the packed corridors.

I sat down to watch the audience watching the film, sitting beside Esperanza who had made that wonderful tripe soup that had nearly choked me twelve years before. There is just no comparison between European and Nicaraguan audiences. There is more drama in the seats than ever appears on the screen. They watched the Glasgow part patiently enough and then, when they saw the first sight of Nicaragua, the place went crazy. They started whistling and bawling. They caught sight of a fragment of Nicaraguan folkloric dancing; another crescendo of noise. They saw something as mundane as the main bus station in Managua with people crushing on to a bus; more screams and whistles. And so it went on; the simple delight of seeing themselves, listening to themselves in their own accent. The intensity of their response, sometimes at such simple scenes which didn't raise a murmur in Europe, made me think of the power of the image and who decides what goes up there. Thank goodness Ken and Sally had refused point-blank to show a dubbed version prepared in Spain.

Afterwards I caught snippets of all sorts of discussions. I caught sight of a friend, Carmen, who seemed too upset to talk, so I just waved. I listened to an ex-soldier talk to a documentary team outside the cinema about the war. Frank, who was shooting a documentary, told me of an argument between two women he got on tape. One said the film would do nothing for reconciliation and she wanted peace. The other replied she only said that because she hadn't lost someone. She too wanted peace and reconciliation, but didn't want to forget. He also filmed a father explaining to his son what he went through. And so it went on.

I spoke to my friend Carmen the next day. She had been a volunteer in the army at the age of nineteen. She was now in her early thirties with a beautiful child. It was impossible to imagine her out fighting in the countryside. She told me she talked all night with her friends about the film and how it reminded them of what they had gone through. Her eyes filled up and she said, 'The truth is there were hundreds of Carlas.'

AS MAKE THE ANGELS WEEP

On my last day in Nicaragua I caught Daniel Ortega, the Sandinista presidential candidate, and his wife Rosario, on the election stump at a run-down market amid all the chaos and excitement of the many hundreds scratching out a living. He worked the crowd beautifully. He was dressed in an almost priestly collarless white shirt. As he joked with the crowd, Rosario threw red petals up in the air which glistened in the sun, and then threw more and more handfuls over Daniel's hair. In between his jokes and promises, Beethoven's 'Ode to Joy' was skilfully faded in and out on the enormous speakers. More flowers arrived, more jokes, more promises, the music built to an emotional crescendo and Daniel was whisked off in a cavalcade, waving to the crowd, in a huge white jeep reminiscent of the Pope mobile. Sure it was the rough and tumble of party politics in the build-up to what was perceived as a close electoral contest. Sure it was wonderful theatre. But it was still bullshit.

In the shadow of their efforts to placate the US and institutions such as the IMF and the World Bank, I found it very difficult to decipher what the Sandinista platform was, and what it could deliver. Reminding the electorate of where real power lay, Nicolas Burns, a US State Department spokesperson, in the week before the elections, warned, 'I would not use the word "democrat" to

xxiii

describe Daniel Ortega . . . He's a Nicaraguan with a past and we're all familiar with that past. Considering his actions against the US in the past, I think we need to remember that . . .'

'Considering his actions *against* the US in the past . . .' It is beyond parody. I can hear the bard mumble in his grave:

> Dressed in a little brief authority
> Most ignorant of what he's most assured
> His glassy essence like an angry ape
> Plays such fantastic tricks before high heaven
> As make the Angels weep.

Perhaps with slightly less finesse, but with no less accuracy, a Managuan taxi driver summed up Nicaraguan history over the last century. 'Look! If you upset the gringos they screw you.' Yes, he thought Aleman was a politician like all the rest, but at least he wouldn't upset the gringos and had good contacts in Miami, which might bring in jobs. Who knows how representative taxi drivers are, but this attitude, plus his criticism of the Sandinista *pinata*, was repeated again and again by many other drivers.

Despite the 'Ode to Joy' and all those petals, despite signing a deal with ex-Contras (now respectfully called the Resistance), despite their vice-presidential candidate who was a well-known cattle producer, despite sounding meeker than lambs, on 22 October 1996, the Sandinistas were defeated by Aleman of the right-wing Liberal Alliance by 51 per cent to 38 per cent.

Out by the airport I got a whiff of the new Nicaragua; in fact, of Nicaragua and beyond. Around 10,000 people, mostly young women, work out there in an area called the *zona franca*, or tax-free zone. I spoke to the manageress of one of the more successful textile plants where women sew up jeans from material imported from China, according to designs drawn in the US, which are then delivered next door to the airport where they are exported, tax free, to the US and sold in supermarket chains. The manageress was totally open. A salesman, usually from Miami, would come down to negotiate. He would have the option of making his order in the Dominican Republic, Haiti, Honduras, El Salvador or Nicaragua. If he didn't get the price he wanted, he was off elsewhere. Her best price for sewing up a pair of jeans was $1.30, and she struggled to understand how the Chinese and Taiwanese factories in adjoining premises could do it for $1.00.

At dinner break I spoke to a fifteen-year-old worker. She worked fifty-five hours a week for $9. Of course, there were no holidays. Of course, you could be fired just like that. Of course, there were no unions. 'You shouldn't get pregnant either, and they like young girls better. A woman at thirty stands up for herself more.' Wearily she shook her head. 'It's not fair,' she said, before walking off slowly to join a knot of friends, to wander back to the factory, to join thousands of others.

I might be accused of being romantic, but I know what I witnessed when I first went to Nicaragua in 1984. What really got to me was an exhilarating sense of 'possibility'; despite all the problems, there was a feeling of ordinary men and women taking their own destiny by the scruff of the neck and saying, 'We're going to do something here!' It was a fantastic feeling to be working alongside these people. I saw this, and I compared it with what I saw in Honduras, El Salvador and Guatemala, where I saw the exact opposite: people frightened and scared, and for good reason.

Oxfam stated that, from its experience in 76 developing countries, Nicaragua was exceptional for the strength of its commitment to development by its people. The World Council of Churches issued a report in 1983 which sums it up for me: 'What we see is a government faced with tremendous problems, some seemingly insuperable, bent on a great experiment which, though precarious and incomplete at many times, provides hope to the poor sectors of society, improves the conditions of education, literacy and health, and for the first time offers the Nicaraguan people a modicum of social justice for all rather than a society offering privilege exclusively to the wealthy and powerful.'

Why should the attempt to build a 'modicum of social justice' attract such incredible violence and so many lies? Ten years of war mutilated this 'great experiment'. For so many that sense of possibility has been destroyed as they now scramble for survival. Nobody can blame them for being cynical, fatalistic, desperate or plain burnt out. The vote for Aleman is perfectly logical. But what is amazing, despite all that US-sponsored violence, is that there are still so many people, so many – and we were lucky to have many of them working in the film with us – who have still not given up. Faces shoot to mind as I write. You could sense something vital and good within them, and no matter what, they would still go on organizing within their communities for that 'modicum of social justice' which is deep within us. The ultimate victory for all those billions of dollars' worth of torture, murder and destruction would have been to extinguish hope itself, and they haven't.

On impulse, before boarding the flight for the Nicaraguan shoot, I bought *Forbes* business magazine (6 November 1995). I came across an article written by Caspar Weinberger, a former US Secretary of State, now working for some corporate consortium, who, in support of the B2 Stealth bomber ($566 million a piece), quoted General Jon Loh, former commander of Air Combat Command: 'I see the B2 as the centrepiece of a . . . strategy that places increasing importance *on projecting immediate responsive power from the US to a regional crisis anywhere in the world.*'

It's a language I now recognize. For 'crisis' read 'struggle for a modicum of social justice' and we are nearer the truth. Most human suffering is not caused by accident, but by huge investment of resources and careful future planning. They are at it again. It was Kundera who wrote: 'The struggle against power is the struggle of memory against forgetting.'

As an idle fancy I wonder how many wee kids at traffic lights could be given a future for the price of one Stealth bomber at 566 million smackers?

In the summer of 1996 the Zapatistas in the most impoverished (but richest in natural resources) Mexican state of Chiapas held a conference called the 'International of Hope' and said: 'Over the ruins of an exhausted system let us construct the world anew with humanity itself at the centre of decision-making.' Little wonder the Argentinian and US advisors are now there today with the Mexican army advising them on counter-insurgency. Little wonder a leaked memo from a leading US bank in New York called for the destruction of the Zapatista movement. All we have to do is look at the experiences of General Smedley D. Butler (in Appendix 1 at the end of this book) to see the same continuous logic unfold from the beginning of this century, to Nicaragua of the eighties and now to Mexico of the nineties. Movements for social justice cannot be allowed to interfere with corporate profit.

For a brief moment the Nicaraguans tried their best to follow what they called 'the logic of the majority', attempting to use their own resources for their own people. Now, more than ever, deregulation, the communications revolution and the mobility of capital mean that many more around the world are joining ranks with a bewildered Commandante Hueso, as the decisions about our lives are made further and further away from any form of democratic control. It is worth perhaps remembering an observation of Noam Chomsky: 'Unless you get to the source of power, which ultimately is investment decisions, other changes are cosmetic and can only take place in a limited way. To challenge the right of investors to determine who lives and who dies, and how they live and die – that would be a significant move towards the Enlightenment ideals. That would be revolutionary.'

Frederick Douglas, a black man, confronted in his day a system that arbitrarily decided who lived and who died: slavery. That little girl in Managua is tied to those traffic lights every bit as firmly as any slave, but with the more subtle bonds of the so-called new economic order and the so-called free market which define her life as worthless. Frederick Douglas summarized his experience: 'Power concedes nothing without demand. It never did and it never will.'

Paul Laverty
November 1996

At the International Venice Film Festival in September 1996 the jury awarded *Carla's Song* the Presidential gold medal of the Italian Senate for the film that best promoted the values of 'civil progress and solidarity'.

In the absence of Ken Loach, Paul Laverty and Sally Hibbin received the award.

Laverty said: 'Thanks for this prize for "civil progress". If we lived in a truly civilized world the two ex-Presidents of the United States, Ronald Reagan and George Bush, would be tried as war criminals for their crimes against humanity . . . there's a bigger chance Scotland might win the World Cup . . . but we live in hope. Thanks.'

Carla's Song was first shown at the Venice Film Festival in September 1996. The cast and crew includes:

GEORGE	Robert Carlyle
CARLA	Oyanka Cabezas
BRADLEY	Scott Glenn
VICTOR	Subash Sing Pall
MCGURK	Stewart Preston
SAMMY	Gary Lewis
GEORGE'S MOTHER	Margaret McAdam
EILEEN	Pamela Turner
MAUREEN	Louise Goodall
RAFAEL	Salvador Espinoza
ANTONIO	Richard Loza
NORMA	Norma Rivera
HARRY	José Meneses
CARLA'S MOTHER	Rosa Amelia López

Production Designer	Martin Johnson
Art Director	Llorenc Miquel
Editor	Jonathan Morris
Photography	Barry Ackroyd
Music	George Fenton
Screenplay	Paul Laverty
Co-producers	Ulrich Felsberg
	Gerardo Herrero
Producer	Sally Hibbin
Director	Ken Loach

A Parallax Picture in co-production with Road Movies Dritte Produktionen and Tornasol Films S.A.

A Channel 4 Films presentation with the support of The Glasgow Film Fund and the Institute of Culture, Nicaragua.

Carla's Song

BUS DEPOT: GLASGOW

A typically grey Glasgow day. Buses leave the depot at the start of the day, wheeling and turning as they make their way into the city.

Titles: GLASGOW 1987.

CITY STREETS

George Lennox (late twenties), bus driver and slightly scruffy, drives his enormous double-decker down a busy thoroughfare. He lets out an enormous yawn. Mischief in his eyes. The driver in a passing bus, grinning widely, waves at George. George waves back.

He pulls up at the next stop. He can see an inspector among the queue.

Two young girls (fourteen or so) get on. One has an obvious mark on her neck. They giggle away. George looks at her very seriously. He points to his own neck and then hers.

GIRL

Whit?

GEORGE

New hygiene rules. Naebody gets on the bus now wi love bites.

3

GIRL

You trying to be funny . . .

GEORGE

There's nuthin funny about Greater Glasgow Transport Executive.

Her mood changes.

Look! There's the inspector.

Two panicked faces turn to see Victor in the queue behind them. George presses the ticket machine quickly.

Right. Hide it.

The young girl smacks one hand under her chin to hide the love bite and snatches the ticket with the other and the two of them run in a scramble up the bus.

Victor, the Indian inspector jumps on and squeezes up beside the windscreen to let the passengers on. He has several posters wrapped up under his arm.

VICTOR

Ah want a word wi you!

He has to wait to let the rest of the passengers embark. An old woman at the end of the queue moves with difficulty to the bus door. She totters precariously and can't quite make the step. Victor is just about to move towards her to give her a hand but is stunned into silence by George.

GEORGE

Hold on a minute darling. I'll lower the bus.

He grabs his handbrake and rocks it back and forth. It makes a loud rasping creaking sound.

Is that low enough?

WOMAN

Oh . . . that's a big help son.

She totters but makes the step quite easily.

4

Victor has his mouth wide open.

> GEORGE
> A' in the mind Victor. Right love, dae ye want a long ticket or a short ticket?

> WOMAN
> I'm gonnie visit ma sister up at the Victoria.

> GEORGE
> Yer cheaper wi a long one then. Here,
> *(pointing to the ticket on the machine)*
>
> hold the end o that and just keep going tae that first seat there.

She takes the end of the ticket and George keeps pressing the ticket machine till the ticket grows longer and longer as the old lady moves inexorably to her seat. She plonks down.

George opens his security panel and leans out towards her. She still has one end of the ticket firmly in her hand. It stretches in a long parabola with the other end still attached to the machine.

> Is that long enough fir ye?

> WOMAN
> Oh it's a big one, son.

> GEORGE
> That's Europe fir ye. I'll ask the inspector to roll it up nice and tight.

Victor has no choice. He stretches his hand to the ticket still protruding from the machine. Just as he is about to touch it, George gives the machine one more quick flick. Victor jumps, and the ticket grows another two inches.

Victor tears it from the machine and starts to roll it up, heading towards the old woman. George is pissing himself.

> WOMAN
> Thanks very much, son.

GEORGE
(*shouting*)

A pleasure, darlin.

*Victor marches back to George who still has the security panel open.
Victor shakes his head at him.*

Whit's up wi you?

Victor unrolls one of the posters from underneath his arm.

VICTOR

That's whit!

*He holds up a grossly exaggerated caricature of a bus inspector
scratching his balls, entitled:* MCGURK – THE SCRATCHER – WANTED
– DEAD OR ALIVE.

He's doon the road and he's after your blood! Gi me that
poster ya numptie . . .

GEORGE

Hey! That's a work of art . . .

VICTOR

McGurk scratchin his baws! You've already got one
suspension under yer belt Picasso . . . just watch yersel . . .

*He reaches over and takes down a copy of the poster which is Sellotaped
above George's head.*

Ah don't know why Ah bother . . . Ah'm tryin to keep yi in a
joab . . .

GEORGE

Sorry Victor. Sometimes I just takes things too far.

*Victor is about to respond but gives up in exasperation. He jumps off as
the last passenger – a really well-built man – pays for his fare as the
ticket roll comes to an end. His ticket has a big red mark through it.*

Oh ya beauty!! Look at that.

MAN

What?

GEORGE

Look, the red mark. That's you then.

MAN

That's me what?

GEORGE

That's you won a turkey. Take that ticket up to Larkfield
depot, ask to speak to Inspector McGurk and claim yer bird.

*Man wanders up the bus examining his ticket. George opens the security
panel and leans out.*

Don't take no for an answer. If they're no aw claimed he gets
to keep them.

The man still looks a bit confused.

WEE WOMAN
(*with the long ticket*)
I expect it's one o they European things.

*Several passengers examine their tickets. The bus moves on through the
traffic.*

CITY STREETS: LATER

*George's bus approaches a queue. As he pulls in the queue moves
towards the door. In the scramble, George notices a young woman skip
past passengers trying to go unnoticed without paying.*

*He watches her take a seat in his mirror until a passenger starts tapping
his security window for her ticket.*

*He watches her again. A man sits beside her. She squeezes up against
her own side as far as is possible.*

*George hesitates, and then drives off. He can hardly take his eyes off
her. She has natural beauty: real presence. She is not from Glasgow –
her clothes are insufficient for the weather and her hair is thick and
black.*

She rests her head against the side of the window as if really done in.

RADIO CONTROL

Alpha 67/ 12 – 41 where are you? Over.

George angrily presses the button on his radio.

GEORGE

Alpha 67/ 12 – 41. I'm just leaving Duke Street. Over.

RADIO CONTROL

You're running thirty minutes late. Over.

He lets go of the radio switch.

GEORGE

This is a bastarding bus, no a helicopter. Over.

A bus travelling in the opposite direction flashes his lights and the driver taps his head.

George looks in the mirror once again at the girl.

Oh shit.

Sure enough, a big burly man, Inspector McGurk, recognizable from the caricature, and scratching himself, waves him down.

George pulls to a halt giving the steering wheel the tiniest of nudges as if swinging into McGurk just to give him the edge of a fright.

McGurk jumps on.

Welcome aboard, Inspector . . . make yersel at home.

MCGURK

Yer late. How come?

GEORGE

The congestion of circulatory traffic around Strathclyde, not to mention gas works, road works, water works, detours, psychopathic taxi drivers . . .

He points out of the window.

. . . one body to one car . . . a ton of metal under each arse . . . You want tae know whit kept yi waiting? Civilization!

McGurk makes his way among the passengers and starts asking for their tickets.

George looks at the girl again in his mirror. McGurk works his way up the bus towards her. She shrinks further into her window.

George can now see him pointing at her. She turns from him. He taps her on the shoulder. She cringes further. The man beside her moves off. McGurk towers over her. She looks humiliated. He takes out his pen, then his notebook.

George can't stand it any longer. He stops the bus. He puts money in the machine and takes a ticket. He marches up the bus towards them.

Here you are, Shylock. You're 300 years late for the Inquisition . . . it's only forty-five pence . . . just leave the lassie alone . . .

George tries to hand her a ticket. McGurk puts his not inconsiderable bulk between them.

MCGURK
Oh no . . . oh no . . . I've got you this time, smart arse . . .

GEORGE
Well don't take it out on her . . .

McGurk continues to write.

Come on . . . gi' her a break . . .

MCGURK
(*to the girl*)
What's your full name?

She cowers further into her seat, deeply intimidated.

GEORGE
Ah don't believe this . . .

Other passengers start to get involved.

WOMAN
Look . . . she's soaking.

2ND WOMAN
She hasie enough claithes oan.

9

She dips into her purse and tries to stretch by McGurk to give her the fare. She can't stretch past.

Here, pet.

> GEORGE
> (*to McGurk*)

Are you listening?

> MCGURK
> (*to the girl*)

I'm going to ask you one more time . . .

> GEORGE

McGurk . . . for God's sake.

The girl sits, bewildered. McGurk checks the time on his watch and begins to write again. George knocks his writing pad with his knuckles.

Hello. Hello . . .

McGurk picks up his radio and dials in.

> MCGURK

Give me the police.

> GEORGE

For 45p!!

> MCGURK

Get back to yer cabin.

> GEORGE

Ya big constipated miserable prick yi . . .

George strides back to his driver's seat. He looks in the mirror as Carla cowers in her seat. He gestures to her that she should run for it.

She leaps up and George snaps the door open. McGurk clumsily lurches for her. Carla skips out as George shuts the door in McGurk's face. People in the bus start clapping.

Carla runs up the street but turns to see a furious McGurk point viciously at George and start writing in his notebook.

CUT

LARKFIELD BUS DEPOT: TRANSPORT MANAGER'S OFFICE: DAY

George, now very smart, strides along a narrow corridor towards a door with a sign 'TRANSPORT MANAGER' written on it. There is one screw through the middle of the sign which is a bit squint. George straightens it up before knocking. He checks his tie. He knocks. There is a grunt from inside.

He opens the door to be confronted by a heavily set powerful character who pins George with his gaze. He flicks an eye towards a seat. George sits down.

The manager's eyes flick back to a hefty report on his desk. He shakes his head as a thick finger turns another page. At last:

> MANAGER
> So the Scratcher got you at last . . .

George coughs nervously.

> (*reading from the report*)
> 'You big, constipated, miserable prick, you.' I don't think you want the job, do you?

> GEORGE
> I need it.

> MANAGER
> You need it like a hole in the head. Right, a week's suspension. Next time you're out. Right, beat it.

> GEORGE
> Thanks.

As George gets to the door the Manager raises his finger.

> MANAGER
> I don't suppose you know anything about a turkey?

George shakes his head.

> That's a pity. That was funny.

STREET OUTSIDE GEORGE'S HOUSE

George crouches down beside his Suzuki 750 and fiddles with a tiny screwdriver trying to reach an inaccessible corner. His hands are covered in grease. Radio Clyde plays on his radio. A news story about Thatcher fainting at the Palace.

A wee boy who lives next door bounces a ball right beside George.

> WEE BOY
> George, gonnie give me a backie? George, gonnie?

George does his best to ignore him.

The front door of a nearby house slams shut as George's mum and his fourteen-year-old sister Eileen come out on to the street.

> MOTHER
> George . . .

> EILEEN
> Ah thought you said yi wer goin tae sort ma hair-dryer? . . .

George unconsciously wipes his greasy fingers on his old shirt.

> MOTHER
> George . . .

> EILEEN
> And . . . who do you thinks gonnie clean that shirt? Sammy phoned . . . five-a-sides. You've still got his sannies . . .

> MOTHER
> George . . . Maureen's phoned yi three times! Come on . . . catch a grip!

George nods and shrinks under the barrage. The two women watch him sink for cover behind his bike. They walk on but after a few steps look over their shoulders. They catch a grin between themselves as they spot him peering just above the bike.

> WEE BOY
> George, gonnie give me a backie . . .

> GEORGE
> Gonnie do me a favour Peter? Hold that for me. Just for five minutes.

George takes his crash helmet from on top of the bike and puts it on

Peter's head. It looks enormous on his tiny body. He then turns it back to front so the mouth piece and visor are to the back of his head and his face is totally enclosed.

George bends down again and struggles with the screwdriver.

GIRL
George Lennox?

George turns to a beautiful pair of legs. He stands up shocked, to face the girl from the bus.

George doesn't know what to say to her. George's hands stick out in front of him like melons.

I got your address from the depot . . . I just wanted to say . . .

GEORGE
Oh don't worry about that . . .

GIRL
Did you lose your job?

GEORGE
A short sabbatical . . .

GIRL
I'm very sorry . . . I brought you this.

She holds out a tiny package, carefully wrapped. George fusses with his dirty hands and doesn't know how to take it. He indicates a breast pocket.

GEORGE
That's awfie nice of yi . . . stick it in here . . .
   (*as she puts it in his pocket*)
Come in for a coffee? Ah've got to wash my hands.

GIRL
No . . . I must go.

GEORGE
Just hang on a minute.

George runs into the house.

13

He washes his hands like a madman, and with a quick squint in the mirror, scampers out.

She's gone. He looks up and down the street.

Where did she go, Peter?

There is a muffled voice behind the helmet.

George turns the corner and sprints down a busy street. He dodges in between prams and shoppers. He stops and runs in the other direction. He's frustrated at not finding her, but pissed off at himself for trying so hard. Athletically he jumps up on to a waste-bin on the side of a lamp-post so that he can see above the heads of shoppers.

He sees her walking away, a hundred yards further off. He jumps down and catches her up outside a café. In the distance, between passing cars, they have an animated conversation. Unheard, but with eloquent body language. He beckons, cajoles . . . charms. She walks on. Stops. He pleads. She hesitates. At last she gives in. He sighs deeply.

A CAFÉ

Old Italian style café and ice-cream shop. Long thin tables and seats with latches are screwed into the floor. The tables and chairs are immovable; each customer is squeezed in beside his or her neighbour. Those opposite really invade body space.

The café is full. This is the domain of taxi drivers who have made this place their local.

The waitress gives them a coffee each.

George and the girl are squeezed up face to face, knee to knee.

George holds up his hand as if to shake hands, but they have only been half washed. He's caught in mid flight. He puts them down again as Carla holds hers up.

> GEORGE
> They're still really manky. George.

> CARLA
> Carla.

There is a wisp of thick black hair just in front of her eye and he has to exercise all his will power not to brush it gently to the side of her face.

They size each other up; eyes first, then hands, hair, cheeks . . . in between flustering with milk and sugar.

Neither are in a rush to say anything. They drink their coffee. There is no accounting for chemistry. Their legs touch accidentally.

GEORGE

Where . . .?

Carla cuts him off.

CARLA

Don't ask me questions. No questions.

More sups of coffee. George picks up the salt cellar.

GEORGE

Map.

He does a rough map of Scotland.

Scotland!

He drops a spot on Glasgow and points to himself triumphantly.

Glasgow!

He gives her the salt-cellar. She hesitates. His ingenuity overcomes her reluctance. She blows the salt over him without a second thought.

She starts drawing a map with the rushing salt. Carla and George concentrate, oblivious to the world. So do four taxi drivers who have all stopped eating.

It's not the clearest map in the world but North America and South America are clearly recognizable. She drops a spot in Central America just as George did for Glasgow.

Africa!

The taxi driver beside him sticks in a big fat finger of explanation:

TAXI DRIVER #1
Naw, ya diddy. That's the States, that's South America, and that's . . . that's the wee bit in the middle . . .

DRIVER #2
Ah once knew a guy from that wee bit in the middle . . .

DRIVER #3
How did ye know where that was, Frank?

DRIVER #2
I'm a taxi driver. Geography's ma livelihood.

They get up to leave and wander out.

Chuck him darlin . . . he's too stupit.

(*in the distance*)
Remember we got Costa Rica in the World Cup.

DRIVER #3
When were yer last fare up the Panama Canal, Frank . . .

DRIVER #2
You're gonnie get a toe up the Panama Canal . . .

George and Carla continue a good look at each other.

> GEORGE

'Carla' . . . Ah like that . . . Ah don't suppose yi've got a second name? . . .

She almost smiles, but then looks strangely sad.

> CARLA

. . . I must go . . .

> GEORGE

Don't.

> CARLA

I'm very sorry about your job . . . I've got to go.

> GEORGE

Why?

> CARLA
> (*sharply*)

Question.

> GEORGE

Finish your coffee . . .
> (*with a glint in his eye*)

you might never see me again . . . and you'll never forgive yourself . . .

> CARLA

I'm sorry.

> GEORGE

So am I.

She gets up to leave. George is thinking desperately.

Right . . . your phone number . . .

She shakes her head.

Ah'm amaaaaazin company!

She hesitates.

Come on!!

She almost gives in.

I'll let you drive ma bus . . .

CARLA

CARLA
334 8249.

She's gone in a second. George instinctively swipes a pen from the pocket of a passing waitress and writes the number on the back of his hand. He pops it back again as she returns. She's unaware each time.

He suddenly remembers the little package she gave him. He pulls it from his pocket and notices how carefully packaged it is. He tears open the paper to reveal a simple folkloric brooch painted by hand in very bright colours of a Central American scene: campesinos *picking corn in the fields with a tiny village in the background. He tosses it up and catches it with a flourish.*

The waitress starts wiping the salt from the table.

WAITRESS
Right Mr Amazin . . . are yi quite finished?

A PUB: THE WEEKEND

George and Sammy (mate from the buses) pick up two enormous trays of drinks and like circus performers delicately fight their way through a phalanx five deep that surrounds the bar.

They place the drinks among a pile of friends. George takes his place beside Maureen. She automatically puts her left hand – with engagement ring visible – on his thigh as he returns, without breaking off the conversation with her friend to the right.

George looks slightly out of it. He takes a big swig from his pint of heavy.

SAMMY
What's up wi you? Yi've hardly said a word aw night . . .

GEORGE
Nuthin.

SAMMY
(*incredulous*)
Nuthin nuthin . . .

*Puts his big arm round George and gives him a huge smacker on the
cheek which almost reverberates.*

. . . tell Uncle Sammy . . .

*Some of their pals just love to see George on the receiving end for a
change.*

GEORGE
Fuck off.

Sammy pulls his chair in closer.

SAMMY
Seriously.

GEORGE
Seriously nuthin.

SAMMY
Is it McGurk? Something tae dae wi work?

George shakes his head.

*Sammy leans over George and catches Maureen's arm who is still in
mid flight with her pal.*

Are you playing hard to get . . .?

MAUREEN
(*to George*)
Whit are you saying to him?

*Sammy is delighted at the mischief. She whacks Sammy in good
sport.*

Ya big cheeky lump . . .

The band breaks into an old romantic favourite.

SAMMY
That's it . . . everybodaaaaaaay!

The table rises as one to the dance floor. Dreams, passionate grips, sweat and sweet perfume. Maureen snuggles into George.

MAUREEN

Forgot to tell yi . . . Alice can make it from Australia . . . yi were right . . . nuthin like a good old fashioned threat . . . Ah think we should stick wi the church hall . . . it's much cheaper . . . but yi're gonnie hiv to start cooperating wi the old monsignor . . . Are you listenin tae me?

GEORGE

Aye . . .

MAUREEN

. . . I just canni stand it when he calls you a 'lapsed' Catholic . . . makes me think yir lungs hiv caved in and yir aw diseased . . . he's quite funny really . . . he even told a knock knock joke . . . but Ah'm sick o turnin up by masel wi aw these 'couples' fir the 'pre-nuptial' class . . . they look at me as if Ah'm a single parent or something . . . well yi know what Ah mean . . . ma maw says it wid be easier marrying a Protestant than you . . . it's a good job you can make her laugh, George Lennox . . .

She pulls back so she can look straight into his face.

Rosemary can git us a big discount wi the flowers . . . and Ah don't give a toss about a fancy car . . . Are you OK?

He nods.

Kiss me.

He draws her tightly to himself, her head against his chest, his hand protectively behind her head. He closes his eyes tightly as if deeply anguished.

GEORGE'S HOUSE: THE SAME NIGHT

The upstairs landing. George's bedroom door opens, he tiptoes out and moves stealthily to another bedroom. He opens the door quietly and sneaks inside.

He gropes around in the semi-dark. He stumbles on a pair of shoes and makes a bit of a clatter.

A body groans while George holds his breath.

Silence again from the body. He finds a bookshelf and peers at the books. He stands up but trips over a stool and falls flat on his face, making an almighty bang.

Eileen, in a frightened start from a deep sleep, sits bolt upright and snaps on the light.

George is on the floor gripping his knee in agony.

EILEEN

I suppose you've got an explanation for this, ya pervert.

GEORGE

That's some place to put a stool.

EILEEN

You're steamin. Mum!

GEORGE

Shush! Where's yer atlas?

EILEEN

Better off with a compass. Yer room's first on the right, George.

GEORGE

Just gi me it.

Eileen leans across to the end of her bed and pulls her school atlas from the shelf. She throws it at him on the ground. It hits him on the knee. He jolts with the pain.

EILEEN

You *are* steamin.

Angrily she turns out the light. George gets up. Once more he stumbles.

GEORGE

Shit!

George arrives in his bedroom, sits on the bed, double pillow, knees up, fingering through the old atlas. He turns to Central America. His finger traces over Guatemala, El Salvador, Honduras, Nicaragua, Costa Rica and Panama.

He mouths the words to himself.

A STREET NEAR GEORGE'S HOUSE

George, in his uniform, is in a phone booth, dialling a number. He fingers a scrap of paper with a number on it. Peter (wee boy with George at the motor bike) on his way to school stops, and just stands beside George. He stares up at him.

> PETER
>
> Who are ye phonin?

> GEORGE
>
> Ma agent.

> PETER
>
> Oh. Are ye gonnie gi me a backie?

> GEORGE
>
> Naw.

> PETER
>
> Why no?

> GEORGE
>
> Instructions.

> PETER
>
> The agent?

> GEORGE
>
> Aye.

George gets the 'unobtainable' tone. He snaps down the receiver. He redials. Again the line is dead. Impatiently George bangs the phone down and steps out.

> PETER
>
> Sounds a right wank if you ask me.

CITY CENTRE: JUNCTION OF BUSY ROAD AND PEDESTRIAN PRECINCT

George drives a totally jam-packed bus along a main street. Even the aisles are full of standing passengers. A grim faced older man with

22

shiny false teeth is the nearest passenger to George.

Just as he's passing the pedestrian precinct George casually looks to his right. He catches the quickest glimpse of a girl who looks like Carla some forty yards away. But he's already past the precinct. He screeches to a halt and all the passengers, especially the older man beside George, are thrown forward.

George slams the bus into reverse and moves backward. The passengers are shaken up and mystified. Horns start pounding. George can see the girl. It is Carla. The horns build to a crescendo. George checks his mirror: angry motorists behind him. He looks at his watch and accelerates forward. The old boy beside him stumbles forward once more. He checks his teeth.

OLDER MAN

Driver! You're a fucking dumpling!

CITY CENTRE: ST VINCENT'S STREET: EVENING

George, in uniform, runs along the street in the direction of the corner by the precinct. He turns the corner and looks south. Carla has gone. He walks up to a news vendor and questions him. The news vendor points to the north side of Buchanan Street precinct. In the distance George can see a sizeable crowd.

George sprints towards them. As he does so the sound of music becomes stronger and stronger. He can distinguish foreign words. Spanish. He bobs and weaves between bodies and finally catches a glimpse of Carla as she dances in the middle of the circle.

George pushes closer. Carla skips, sweeps and arches with a gentle elegance as if in her own private world. There's not a sound from the crowd who are struck by her intensity, almost a sadness. It touches George deeply. The tape comes to an end. There is a moment of silence before the crowd claps enthusiastically and throws coins into a hat. She zips on a jacket and shyly keeps her eyes to the ground.

George pushes his way closer. She catches sight of him. She snaps up her recorder and hat (although people are still contributing) and sprints off.

Frustrated, George is caught between bodies as she disappears.

GEORGE

Carla! Carla!

He sees her turn a corner and tears after her.

A STREET AND HOSTEL

George catches up with Carla. They are both totally puffed out.

GEORGE

Carla . . . Carla!! Will yi wait just a minute . . .

She swings round.

CARLA

Just leave me alone. Go home, George . . .

GEORGE

Ah don't understand . . .

CARLA

I'm not asking you to understand . . .

GEORGE

Why did you give me that bum number . . .

CARLA

Why did you ask? Just leave me alone.

She stops outside a run-down hostel. The entrance is horrible and seedy. Smell of stifling disinfectant. Poverty. George realizes this is where she is staying.

GEORGE

Whit are you doing here?

Carla, exasperated, passes through swing doors and takes out her keys to open another within.

George skips through the swing door on impulse.

There is a huge sign 'WOMEN ONLY'.

CARLA
(*furious*)

Only Women! If I'm caught with you I get kicked out.

Not till . . .

CARLA
(*whispering violently*)
She's coming . . . get out now . . .

*They both hear the warder walking along the corridor towards the
security kiosk. She's whistling! The sash!*

(*nervously staring at the security window*)
Out!

GEORGE
Not till yi speak to me.

Whistling and footsteps are almost upon them.

CARLA
I need this place.

*George ducks down on his knees, up tight against the wall, a split
second before the big face of an intimidating female warder peers from
the window.*

WARDER
Lost yer keys again?

CARLA
I'm OK.

She opens the door and George skips through at her feet.

INSIDE THE HOSTEL

*Carla and George make their way along a miserable corridor with worn
brown linoleum. Doors line each side. The walls don't go all the way up
to the ceiling; cubicles rather than rooms. The lighting is barely adequate
and one strip light by Carla's door flashes in malfunction. The sound-
proofing is non-existent and the occasional shout can be heard.*

*Carla fumbles for her key; her face flashes up (as does her anger)
intermittently with the faulty light.*

Who do you think you are?

(*in Spanish*)

Son of a bitch, I don't believe this.

She throws open her door. She turns on another strip light to reveal a pokey horrible cubicle; one narrow metal-framed bed, a tiny desk, a shiny brown chair. A rucksack in a corner. A couple of odds and ends.

GEORGE

Jesus . . . Carla. This is a nightmare.

He picks up a letter that has fallen on the floor by the bed and holds it up to her.

With a vicious swipe, she whacks George on the face with the full weight of the tape-recorder. George's nose bursts with the collision and streams with blood. She kicks and punches him like a woman possessed as George cowers in the corner, riding the blows. Her punches slow down till she collapses on the floor. Her entire body trembles in uncontrollable, barely audible sobs. Deep quiet sobs. Not tears. Desperate, painful heart-broken done-in sobbing.

Oh Christ. I'm so sorry. Really sorry.

He doesn't know what the hell to do. He sniffs trying to control the flow of blood. He kneels down beside her and tentatively he puts a hand on her shoulder. The sobs still rack her body.

He looks around him. The wooden partition in front of him has a striking magazine photograph stuck up with tacks of two huge volcano peaks side by side. One edge of the photo is ragged.

He can hear voices mumble next door. Heavy steps march along the corridor.

WARDER

What the hell's going on in there?

Carla jumps. The warder pounds the door.

Open up or I'll kick this fucking door aff its hinges.

George smartly opens the door just as the big warder is about to take a running kick at the door. She stares at George's bloody nose.

Who the fuck are you?

GEORGE

I'm her spiritual advisor.

WARDER

. . . and Ah suppose that's stigmata . . .

She makes a move for him.

GEORGE

Easy . . . if Ah lose anymore Ah'll need a transfusion . . .

WARDER

Right . . . penis face . . . out! That goes fir you too, sweetheart . . . you knew the golden rule . . .

GEORGE

Jesus . . . it's ma fault . . .

WARDER

It always is . . .

GEORGE

Listen . . . Ah sneaked ma way in . . .

WARDER

Santa Claus? . . . down the chimney? . . .

GEORGE

It's no her fault . . . right . . . Ah barged ma way in . . .

WARDER

Naebody . . . naebody barges past me . . . especially 'men' . . . I want yi baith oot o here in five minutes or Ah'll call the polis . . .

GEORGE

Yir no listenin . . .

WARDER

Correct. Four minutes.

She about turns and waddles down the corridor. Faces of women peer at George from every door.

George gently closes the door, frightened to antagonize her further.

GEORGE

Right, Carla . . . come on, I'm taking yi out of here . . . some place safe . . .

He helps her up from the ground. She wipes the tears from her eyes. He starts stuffing her clothes and few bits and pieces into her rucksack. She has very little.

Is this all yi have, Carla?

She nods. She starts to help him. George is about to close the top of the rucksack when Carla hesitates. She then lifts up the mattress to reveal dozens of letters. She gathers them up. George notices the foreign stamps.

They are all unopened, which draws his attention.

He closes the rucksack. Carla moves to the wall and tries to undo the tacks around the picture of the volcano. She can't even manage that, and turns to lean her back against the wall. She really looks done in.

It's OK.

He takes down the photo and handles it carefully.

STREET OUTSIDE THE HOSTEL

They emerge from the hostel, George carrying Carla's bag. He runs to the kerb to hail a passing taxi. He gives the driver an address and they climb in.

Carla lays her head meekly against the window. George looks at her: eyes closed, she leans her head against the partly opened window, exposing her slender neck.

Her fragility somehow moves him. He gently feels his bloody nose. He catches sight of the taxi driver watching him carefully in the mirror.

SAMMY'S FLAT: AN OLD TENEMENT

The taxi pulls up in front of an old red stone tenement building. They get out. George pays and they enter the block. George carries Carla's rucksack and recorder.

Carla looks hesitant as they climb the stairs. George marches on and stops outside a door. He pulls a metal handle and an old bell rings inside. He nods to Carla trying to give her confidence.

The door opens. It is Sammy, bleary-eyed, with a towel around his waist. He scowls at George's bloody nose and Carla by his side.

> GEORGE
>
> Carla, Sammy. Sammy, Carla.

> SAMMY
>
> Whit the fuck are you . . .?

> GEORGE
> (*to Sammy*)
>
> Trust me.

> (*barging past, to Carla*)
>
> This way.

He leads Carla through to Sammy's back bedroom and dumps her rucksack on an old settee.

> We'll soon have this dump tidied up. Don't you worry.

> SAMMY
>
> Aye. We can start straight away if yi like.

> GEORGE
>
> Carla, I'll be with you in a minute.

He leaves and closes the door behind him and walks into the kitchen. Sammy follows. His towel falls to reveal a bare arse in hot pursuit. He grabs the towel round his bollocks.

> (*putting on the kettle*)
>
> Don't jump tae conclusions.

SAMMY

Me! Conclusions! Jesoh! It's the bridesmaid int'it? Naw . . .
it's Maureen's pen pal! Ah! The mither-in-law wi a face lift
and a new hair-do . . . Far be it from me,
                    (*tightening his towel*)
'the *best man*', to jump to fuckin' unreasonable
conclusions . . .

GEORGE

It's no like that Sammy . . . Ah'm just tryin to help her
oot . . .

SAMMY

A damsel in distress! Right, Mother Teresa . . . just make
yersel at home. Gi me a wee shout in the mornin . . . and
we'll have a little 'chat' if it isnie too much trouble.

THE BEDROOM: SAMMY'S FLAT

*George tentatively hands Carla a cup of tea. She looks cold. He takes
off his jacket and puts it round her. He takes a sip of tea and sniffs. His
nose bleeds slightly.*

CARLA

You dive into things without thinking . . .

GEORGE

Carla . . . I'm really sorry . . . yi can stay here as long as yi
like . . . Sammy's ma best mate . . .

CARLA

Does everyone do as you ask George? Is your life so simple?

*He looks crushed. She takes a tissue from her pocket and unexpectedly
leans across, gently wiping the trickle of blood from his nose.*

CARLA

How's your nose?

GEORGE

Still breathing . . .

She smiles which gives him encouragement.

CARLA

I suppose we're almost equal . . . I nearly get you kicked out
of your job . . .

GEORGE

And I get you kicked out of yer home . . .

*She wipes his nose again. He stares into her eyes. They catch each
other's look for a moment.*

CARLA

Nicaragua . . . that's . . .

She hesitates.

GEORGE

. . . yer home?

CARLA

. . . where I come from . . .

Something about her delivery stops George from asking any more.

GEORGE

You look exhausted, Carla . . . Hiv a right good long lie and
Ah'll see yi tomorra . . .

He gets up to leave.
. . . whit are you smilin at?

CARLA

I hope it isn't broken . . .

GEORGE

It woudnie be the first time . . .

CARLA

Nor the last . . . Crazy Driver.

He catches mischief in her eye for the first time and grins.

GEORGE

Crazy Dancer!

She watches him close the door.

BUS STOP: LATER

George walks up to a bus stop and stamps his feet and rubs his hands against the cold. He looks pensive but can't help a wry grin breaking through as a drunk beside him, leaning on the pole, finishes off singing a Negro spiritual to his pudding supper.

DRUNK

Nobody knows the troubles Ah've seen, nobody knows but Jesus
> (*bowing his head at the holy word*)

Nobody knows the troubles ah've seen, Glory allelujah!

He catches George's eye.

See bus drivers. Ah love bus drivers.

He offers George a chip, which he takes gratefully.

GEORGE

Thanks, Chief.

DRUNK

Hiv a wee dod of ma black pudding . . . sharin is whit it's aw aboot . . . What goes through yir mind, young man?

As he stretches over the supper slips out of his hand and flips over perfectly to land in a puddle by the kerb.

> (*staring at it*)

That's the story o' ma fucking life.

George stares at the splattered contents.

GEORGE

What will Ah tell Maureen?

DRUNK

Ah had three pickled onions in wi that as a wee treat.

GEORGE

Ah'll just tell her the truth.

A car whizzes by and flattens the supper.

They look up to catch each other's eye.

DRUNK
It's a bastard. In'it?

THE STREETS

A bus, George's, draws away from a stop. A taxi nips in front of him as George pulls out. The bus breaks its tail lights. Both drivers pull to a halt.

The taxi driver jumps out of his taxi, takes one quick look at the end of his vehicle, and starts shouting and bawling at George and giving him the fingers.

George opens the window.

GEORGE
Ah said I was sorry. We'll get . . .

TAXI DRIVER
Blind bastard . . .

Taxi driver, in a rage, spits at George. George slams the window shut. He is really pissed off at the wanton aggression.

The big taxi driver is still on the prowl, like a wild animal. George opens the bus door and beckons him in. Taxi driver jumps on, spoiling for another go. George closes the door, rams the bus into gear, overtakes the taxi and accelerates up the road. Taxi driver starts hammering on the security window, jumping around and wildly looking back trying to see what is happening to his taxi.

George turns on his radio to contact the control room.

GEORGE
Have a listen to this . . .

The taxi driver still pounds on the security window.

TAXI DRIVER
You're deid, pal . . . mince-meat . . . kaput . . . ya sheep-shaggin . . . bus *driveeeers*!!!!

George holds a hand to his ear pretending he can't hear through the security window which makes the driver foam at the mouth with utter rage.

33

George sails past a bus stop despite the fact that twelve arms are extended. The whole bus now looks backwards at the queue.

At last George pulls to a halt, nowhere near a bus stop, and opens the door. He puts his head in his hands and leans on the steering wheel. The taxi driver is first off, swearing, followed slowly by the other passengers. Two wee women give him a sympathetic look.

>   OLD WOMAN
> Are you OK, son?

STREET OUTSIDE SAMMY'S FLAT

The sound of the hooter precedes the bus as George pulls up outside Sammy's tenement building. Heads peer down from windows.

George jumps from the cab and dives into Sammy's close. One or two kids gather round the bus.

Moments later, George leads a bewildered Carla out of the tenement and into the bus. He starts the engine and drives off. The kids are left gazing in awe.

Carla looks round at the empty bus. She stands up beside him at his security window which is open.

>   CARLA
> Where do we go?

>   GEORGE
>   (*indicating the sign*)
> No passengers beyond this point, madam . . .

>   CARLA
> What do you do?

>   GEORGE
> (*turning a tight corner where the bus should obviously not be*)
> In the interests of road safety, madam, please do not distract
> the driver in the course of complicated manoeuvres . . .

>   CARLA
> George?

GEORGE

Madam?

CARLA

Are you crazy?

He grins like a loony.

NARROW COUNTRY LANE

George drops the bus into the lowest gear to negotiate a very steep hill on a very narrow road between Balmaha and Rowerdennan (forty-five minutes north of Glasgow). Several campers give the passing bus an incredulous look. The bus gets to the brow of the hill to reveal a stunning view of Loch Lomond, a string of mountains to their left and a string of mountains to the right, the tallest of which is Ben Lomond.

George takes a sudden swing off to the left and heads down a very rough tractor track. The bus sways dangerously as it smacks into each pothole. Carla looks at George as if he has gone crackers.

Suddenly the radio crackles. They catch each other's eye.

CONTROL ROOM
(*woman's voice*)

34/ 79 – 24 . . . are you receiving me? Please make contact as soon as possible . . .

George grabs a bag of crisps from Carla and flicks on the radio. He crushes the bag of crisps into the microphone as Control repeats the message.

GEORGE
(*as he continues crushing the bag violently*)

Corner of . . . are . . . receiving . . . confirm. How many times . . . contact . . . corner of . . . McGurk's a poxy bastard . . . one more time . . . corner of . . . please make contact as soon as possible.

Carla cannot hide a smirk.

George switches off the radio and swings into a dead end, overlooking the loch. The bus is in between some bushes, hidden from the main road.

35

They climb out of the bus.

> GEORGE
> (*examining the bus*)
> That should do it. Right, we're going up there.

> CARLA
> You go up there?

> GEORGE
> A little exercise never hurt anyone.

> CARLA
> That's a mountain.

> GEORGE
> Trust me.

BEN LOMOND

Two tiny bodies in the distance make their way up a steep path.

Carla sings a famous Latin American song called 'Vientos del Pueblo' by Victor Jara (the Chilean singer-songwriter who had his hands crushed by Pinochet's soldiers and thereafter disappeared from the stadium, where the prisoners were being held).

It doesn't matter that George can't understand the words. She sings it with her whole heart and soul, truly haunting and moving.

Various shots of them as they move up the mountain. Stopping, speaking, watching, listening with the attention of first-time lovers. Stunning views in the distance; and the beauty of Loch Lomond.

Carla turns to look at what seems like the whole of the world. Tears roll down her cheeks. George takes her by the hand for the first time.

> GEORGE
> (*with obvious love for the place*)
> That's Ben Lomond up there . . . and Loch Lomond down there . . . it goes on for miles . . . Ah've been up here hundreds of times . . . Ah first came here wi ma Grandpa . . . when Ah was just a kid. He loved this place. Know whit gets me? It's never the same! There's always a wee surprise . . .

36

the light, the water, the speed o' the clouds . . . a sky-lark . . .
a storm. Just look at the colour o' these ferns . . . and there's
never ever ever any big orange buses!

> (*looking out over the loch*)

When Ah'm pissed off . . . it makes me peaceful . . . when
Ah'm happy . . . it makes me mair happy! It does something
to yi . . . Ah canni explain, Carla . . .

*George opens up his haversack and takes out food including a bottle of
champagne. He hands Carla two transparent plastic cups.*

Oh ya beauty!!

The top comes flying off and champagne sprays them both.

*They sit down on a rock, snuggling up beside each other in the wind as
they get tucked in.*

*Carla holds up her glass and stares at the bubbles in the light. She
inhales deeply.*

GEORGE
Right . . . who do you want to toast?

She shrinks into herself.

> (*holding up his cup*)

Come on . . . it'll bring 'em good luck!

> (*drawing it out of her, whispering*)

. . . they might even hear us from up here if yi whisper it . . .

*She slowly lifts her cup to his as if powered by George's outstretched
toast. The bubbles still sparkle away inside.*

CARLA
> (*slowly*)

To all my family . . . to all my friends, to their safety, to all
their work . . . to the band I played with, to their music . . .

> (*almost overcome*)

. . . to their dreams.

GEORGE
That's lovely . . .

Long pause as Carla tosses the drink around in the cup.

CARLA

. . . and to Antonio wherever he is . . .

GEORGE

Is he your boyfriend?

CARLA

He was . . . and to Nicaragua Libre! . . .

She looks from the bubbles to George's puzzled face.

Free Nicaragua.

George nods to their drinks.

GEORGE

In a oner! Nicaragua Libre!!

They both gulp down their glasses. Carla's eyes water with the gassiness of the bubbles.

CARLA

Oh . . . up my nose!

GEORGE

Yahoooooooooo!

She leans across, picks up the bottle, fills both glasses to the very brim and carefully lays down the bottle.

CARLA

Your turn, driver!

She holds up her glass. He catches the life in her eye.

GEORGE

I'm gonnie toast you.

The fun drains from her face.

GEORGE

Dinae be sad . . . Ah'm no askin anything off yi and Ah don't expect anything . . .

CARLA

You don't know me . . .

GEORGE

Ah know whit Ah feel . . . and whit Ah feel is good . . . dinae be frightened of making people feel so good . . .
        (indicating their drinks)
. . . here's to you . . . and all this . . .
        (a quick indication of the beauty all around them)

CARLA

In a 'oner'?!

GEORGE
(chuckling)

Yeah. In a *oner*!

They gulp them down again. They cuddle in closer. She puts her hand on his knee. He covers it with his own, and they tilt in together.

A TRACK BY LOCH LOMOND

The bus stands forlorn and isolated in pouring rain. George and Carla, already soaked by the sudden shower, run towards it.

George sees that the wheels have sunk into the soft ground.

GEORGE

Holieeeee shit.

He jumps into the cabin, starts the engine and puts it in gear. The wheels spin round in the mud. Carla watches from the platform. George abandons the attempt and they both run upstairs, hair plastered to their faces.

They sit on the upper deck, opposite each other, feet into the aisle. They have a grandstand view of the loch and watch the clouds and rain streak across the sky between mountain ranges. The rain begins to hammer on the bus top.

CARLA

Four seasons in one day . . . very strange.

They pull off their soaking jackets. Carla chatters even more with the cold. George rubs her shoulders and arms to keep warm.

Their faces move closer and closer. They kiss gently. They part for a second. They hold fingertips; another gentle kiss. Harder.

They kiss again. In a flash they kiss madly as the rain pounds down. On their knees; then rolling on the deck in the space at the front. Over

and over they roll: heads under seats, dirt sticking to their wet clothes,
shivering between passion and cold. Glorious raw uncalculated
youthful passion. Bruised lips, who gives a flying fuck. A once in a
lifetime kiss.

The radio crackles from the driver's cab below.

> CONTROL ROOM
> (*deep voice of a man*)
> 34/ 79 – 24 . . . This is the transport manager . . . for the last
> time . . . wherever you are . . . make contact immediately. Ye
> can't hide forever ya bastard.

They kiss again . . . Outside the rain pelts down on the bus.

BUS DEPOT: MANAGER'S OFFICE

George sits on one side of a long table confronting the Transport
Manager and Inspector McGurk.

> TRANSPORT MANAGER
> Have you any idea how many tractors it took . . . pardon my
> language, Mr Lennox, tae get that fucking bus oot o that bog
> . . . Go on. Guess.

> GEORGE
> Two?

Manager shifts his hand to indicate 'higher'.

> Three?

The hand again.

> Four . . .?

> MCGURK
> Would it be too much to inconvenience yer good-self for a
> wee explanation?

George coughs nervously.

> MANAGER
> I'm all ears.

GEORGE

It's quite difficult to put into words . . .

MANAGER

Ah can imagine.

BUS DEPOT: A FEW MINUTES LATER

George walks from the depot. Maureen meets a down-beat George.

MAUREEN

How did it go?

GEORGE

They'll write with their decision. I don't care, Maureen.
Listen, I've got tae talk to ye.

KELVINGROVE PARK

George and Maureen are already in deep conversation and distress.
They rub brows. Their faces are tear stained. She kicks his shin bone
repeatedly.

MAUREEN

How long hiv yi been seeing her?

GEORGE

Ah've just met her a few times . . .

MAUREEN

Hiv yi slept wi her?

GEORGE

Naw . . .

MAUREEN

Did yi want tae?

GEORGE

Maureen . . .

MAUREEN

Yi've never ever lied tae me . . .

42

GEORGE

Probably . . . but Ah hardly know her . . .

MAUREEN

Just think what yer throwin' away.

GEORGE

Oh Maureen . . . I canni live wi this . . .

MAUREEN

Live wi what?

GEORGE

Oh Christ . . .

MAUREEN

George. The truth.

GEORGE

Maureen. Yer ma best pal . . . but Ah don't want to marry ye
. . . Ah've tried to kid masel oan . . . but Ah canni . . .

MAUREEN

My God . . . yi mean it.

GEORGE

Ah wish Ah didnie . . . but it's the truth.

*She angrily shakes his hands from her and walks off for three yards. She
turns round to him again and they both hug tightly.*

GEORGE'S BEDROOM: MORNING

*Eileen bursts into George's bedroom with a letter. She throws open the
curtain. He hardly moves. Open distaste at the clothes on the floor.
She violently pulls the pillow from underneath him and whacks him
with it.*

EILEEN

You've got to get your act together!

GEORGE

What's up wi you?

EILEEN

You know whit's up wi me. Yer whole life's a total
disaster . . .

GEORGE

You're just fourteen. So shut yer trap . . .

He notices the letter.

Oh naw . . .

EILEEN

Can Ah open it?

George pulls the pillow over his head. Eileen rips open the letter.

'Dear Mr George Lennox, Following the extraction of a sixty-
nine-seater double decker bus from a Loch Lomond bog on
Tuesday last' . . . George! I thought you said you were
involved in a little accident . . .

GEORGE
(*lifting up one end of the pillow*)
Ah 'accidentally' got stuck in a bog . . .

EILEEN

. . . 'and after careful examination of your appalling
disciplinary record, the unanimous decision of the panel is to
terminate forthwith your contract of employment with
Greater Glasgow Transport Executive . . . Yours sincerely,
Angus McConnel, Transport Manager' . . . He's put in a wee
note in pencil . . .

She reads it hesitantly.
. . . 'Lennox, ya daft bastard, if you're totally stuck, get back
to me in six months . . . but it's probably for the best. Angus
. . . P.S. I hear the Soviet Union are still looking for
astronauts.'

*Eileen in some shock sits on the bed beside him and gently pulls the
pillow from over his head.*

EILEEN

What are you going to do?

His mind is already racing. He catches sight of her worried face.

> GEORGE

Don't you fret, Eileen, OK.

STREET, CLOSE AND ENTRANCE TO SAMMY'S FLAT

An animated George runs along the street, skips into the close and pants up the last flight of steps. He momentarily stops at Sammy's door which lies half open. The hallway is full of envelopes with foreign stamps ripped open and scattered all over.

> GEORGE

Carla? Sammy? Anyone home?

Absolute silence. George, perturbed, moves quickly from one room to another. Carla's door is shut.

Carla? Are you there?

He knocks. No answer. He opens the door. More envelopes. The room is in a shambles.

George becomes aware of the running water and moves towards the bathroom.

Carla? Carla?

Still no answer. He knocks the door. Nothing.

He hesitates, then turns and tries the door. Locked. He calls her name, then suddenly kicks the bathroom door as hard as he can.

Carla lies in an overrunning bath, red with her own blood. Her arm, neck and hair slouch over the side of the bath. Pages of letters float around her. Some have floated off with the water and now stick to the floor. She doesn't move.

George whimpers for a second. In a split second he has pulled out the plug; sucking sound as if her very life is being drawn from her. He leans into the bloody water and lifts her out. The letters floating on the surface stick to her body as he pulls her clear of the water and lays her on the floor. There are no signs of life.

Sweet Jesus . . .

He tries to feel for a pulse. Nothing.

We hear George's steps run to the phone, dialling and muffled sounds.

Carla's pale body lies motionless; the soggy letters hiding her nakedness; the almost deafening sound of the water gurgling and groaning down the plug-hole.

George sprints back in and kneels at her head.

> Oh . . . for fuck's sake don't die on me. Carla! Carla!

He begins desperate mouth to mouth resuscitation as the last few inches of escaping water reaches its noisy crescendo.

Her face has a blue sheen.

CITY STREETS

An ambulance hustles down a street of tenement houses, lights flashing. It turns the corner into a main road and is lost in the traffic.

HOSPITAL: INTENSIVE CARE: LATER

George sits with his head in his hands by the swing door outside the intensive care ward. Doctors and nurses swish back and forward. George can occasionally catch a glimpse of her bed as the door swings open. He can only concentrate on the swishing sound of the door as it oscillates back and forth. Back and forth. Back and forth. In his hand is the brooch that Carla gave him. He turns it over and studies it.

He can see medics around her. The consultant, the registrar, a no-nonsense sister and a young medic who looks dead on his feet.

George looks through the window. The medics finish their conversation. The sister suddenly appears at the window in front of George, much to his embarrassment. He notices a fairly big crucifix around her neck.

GEORGE

Can I see her?

SISTER

Ye're not family.

George looks done in.

46

Right, two minutes, and ye better be gone by the time I get back. Ask him.

George moves towards the young doctor who is just about to leave Carla.

GEORGE

How is she?

DOCTOR

We'll have to see if she comes round.

GEORGE

Just tell me the truth.

The young doctor looks exhausted. George touches his arm.

DOCTOR

Well . . . it's close. Too close for comfort. The next twenty-four hours are critical.

GEORGE

Oh Jesus . . . Carla.

George grips the bed beside her.

DOCTOR

Listen, how well do you know her?

GEORGE

Ah know this sounds daft . . . Ah don't know her well, but I'm close . . . I just care . . . yi've got to tell me . . .

DOCTOR

Listen . . . this is all confidential . . . if she finds out . . .
(*indicating the sister*)
. . . she'll have my bollocks . . . this is her second time . . .

GEORGE

Naw!

DOCTOR

About six weeks ago. I was on then too. She's been through the mill . . .

His buzzer bleeps continuously.

47

Sorry, I've got to go.

George looks over his shoulder at a nurse at the bottom end of the ward with his back to him, then picks up Carla's file and sits down.

He looks down at the file. He flicks through it nervously, his hands shaking.

CARLA DELGADO; AGE 27 YEARS. NICARAGUAN – TEMPORARY RESIDENCY IN BRITAIN. STATUS – TO BE DECIDED BY HOME OFFICE.

George flicks through the title pages of a couple of weighty reports by consultant psychologists. Each is headed POST TRAUMATIC STRESS SYNDROME.

George's eyes scan the paragraphs as he nervously tries to keep an eye on the sister.

GEORGE
(*voice-over*)
'Carla is highly articulate with an above average IQ. She learnt English in Miami during a six-month spell with her uncle. Her mother forced her to leave Nicaragua against her will after her elder brother was murdered by Somoza's National Guard. She returned home after the revolution in July of 1979.'

'. . . she soon graduated through the ranks and was a key figure in co-ordinating the literacy campaigns instigated by the Sandinistas.

'. . . She volunteered to work in remote mountain areas which were increasingly attacked by the Contra.'

Sister walks towards him and stands at the other side of the bed. George freezes.

SISTER
Right, that's it. Come on.

GEORGE
Sister, Ah've only got one more decade to go . . . to finish ma rosary . . . please.

Sister's belligerence immediately eases.

                         SISTER
    God bless you, son.

George flicks to the report once again.

                         GEORGE
                       (*voice-over*)
    '. . . on the 11th August that year a brigade was caught in a
    Contra ambush.'
                       (*out loud*)
    Oh my God . . . '. . . Due to extreme stress on her part it was
    pointless at this stage in the first interview . . .'

George muffles his mouth with his hand; then, to himself:

    What is this . . . '. . . Carla repeatedly mentions a young man
    called Antonio . . .'

George flicks through a few pages and sees the name ANTONIO
highlighted throughout the report with a yellow marker.

George puts the report back. He takes her by the hand.

    For fuck's sake . . . Holy Christ . . . Carla . . . why could ye
    no tell me . . .?

*The sister comes behind him and gently lifts him up. She too can only
hug him.*

    Ah've got tae come back straight away . . . ye see . . . she's
    got this stupit wee . . . fucking photie . . . o' a volcano . . . it's
    only this size . . . it's no even framed . . . if she makes it . . .
    it's got to be here on her wall. It's got tae be . . .

STREETS

*George is riding on the passenger platform of a bus as it speeds along.
He jumps off before it reaches a stop, crosses the road, and is soon lost in
the traffic and pedestrians.*

SAMMY'S FLAT

*George runs up the stairs, two at a time, and beats on Sammy's door.
Sammy opens it.*

                           49

SAMMY

How is she?

George looks really upset. Out of breath, he can hardly speak.

SAMMY

She's no . . .

GEORGE

Naw . . .

George bursts past him to Carla's bedroom and goes to the magazine picture on the wall. He starts to take it down, with great care.

SAMMY

Ah tried to save they letters . . . they're smudged tae fuck . . . poor wee soul . . .

George rolls up the poster as he follows Sammy into the kitchen.

Sammy has nailed three rows of string to the wall. Dozens of sheets of paper, dangling from the string by clothes pegs, waft gently, caught in the rising heat. The sheets, stained red with Carla's blood, are now crisp and dry, but the writing on them appears irreparably smudged by the water.

George looks closely at two sheets. They are still legible. He can't read them because they are in Spanish. He takes them down carefully, and puts them in his wallet.

HOSPITAL: EARLY MORNING

Carla's eyes blink. She opens her eyes. She stares in amazement at her volcano picture in its frame hanging straight in front of her from the privacy curtain rails that surround her bed. The curtains are drawn. It is perfectly silent and almost intimate.

She looks down to the side of her bed to see George on a seat, tucked in tight beside the bed, his face leaning on the blanket towards her, fast asleep.

She gently lifts her hand and puts her finger through his hair and catches a curl. He stirs, and then sits upright, coming to. He holds her hand. Tries to say something but shakes his head.

50

CARLA

George Lennox.

GEORGE

Ah thought Ah'd lost yi, Carla . . .

He's overcome. She puts a finger to his lips. He jumps up and gives her a big cuddle. She gently lifts an arm round him as tears come to her eyes.

The same sister swishes back the curtain and George sits back trying to hide his emotion. Without saying anything and with some warmth she examines Carla.

SISTER
(*in response to George's worried look*)
Yer gonnie hiv tae look after her . . . giv her a week and she'll be up and about . . .

SAMMY'S FLAT

George gently helps Carla up the stairs. He pushes open the unlocked door and guides her through.

A huge sign 'BIENVENIDA CARLA' greets them as Sammy comes from the kitchen to give her a hug. He is wearing a very dainty apron and holding a huge wooden spoon.

Eagerly, Sammy and George urge her to go into her bedroom. She opens the door. The sun streams in through the window. The room is completely redecorated. A total transformation. The bed has a new cover; fresh flowers, and delicate lace curtains. Carla stands in the doorway, taking it all in. She is really touched. George and Sammy look on like schoolboys. Sammy is chuffed but embarrassed.

CARLA

It's beautiful . . . so beautiful . . . the nicest I've ever had . . .

She turns round to face them. Sammy shuffles awkwardly and clears his throat.

SAMMY

It was nuthin . . .

GEORGE

Come on . . . Sammy Van Gogh . . . He even sewed the curtains.

SAMMY

Fuck off you.

Carla stands in front of him and stretches up to give him a kiss on his grizzly cheek.

Ah'd hiv shaved if Ah a knew Ah wuz gettin a snog . . . shit . . . ma lasagna . . .

He disappears. Carla and George laugh and hold each other close.

KELVINGROVE PARK: BY THE RIVER: A WEEK LATER

George and Carla stroll gently by the river. Toddlers throw bread to the ducks and nuts to the squirrels. A four-year-old delights in mastering her new bike.

CARLA

There are some things I must tell you . . .

She looks perturbed.

GEORGE

What is it, Carla?

A toddler falls over beside her. She rushes to the child and picks him up confidently with a string of tender Spanish diminutives. She puts him back down again as his tiny fists grip her fingers for balance. She walks him along some five yards to the tot's elder sister.

George joins her.

She begins to look upset again. George can't take it.

Yi've got nuthin to say to me. Nae questions, nae explanations. We'll put this behind us . . . FOR EVER. Right?

CARLA

You don't . . .

GEORGE

(*cutting her off more sharply, and squeezing her shoulder*)
Right!

Carla relinquishes and they both cuddle in.

SAMMY'S FLAT: CARLA'S BEDROOM: NIGHT

Only the city lights from the open curtains, and perhaps a candle.
George sits on the edge of the bed. Carla sits astride him, both fully
clothed.

George touches her hair as she has her hands around his neck.

CARLA

Touch my face.

George caresses her face with his finger-tips.

No hands.

Intrigued, he kisses her face.

Carla touches his face with her lips, hovering over every little groove
and bump.

She now kisses him, attacking him madly as if trying to exorcise some
insane spirit within her.

GEORGE

Jeesoh . . . Carla!

She moves to whip off his jumper. George takes her arm.

(*mischievously*)
No hands, you said.

He holds the sleeve of her jumper in his mouth. She pulls. Quickly with
the other arm in the same manner. Leaning behind her neck he grips the
back collar of her jumper in his teeth. She pulls it and slides if off. She
does the same with George's jumper, the two ever more urgent.

They both stand up, whipping their shoes off with their feet. George
stands on the toe of one sock and whips if off with the panache of a
toreador. The same with the left sock. Carla giggles.

Carla puts her hand to the belt of his trousers.

GEORGE

No hands.

She sits on the bed. She undoes his belt with her teeth.

George stands on the tips of her tights at her toes. She stretches her legs back and the tights stretch further. George bends down and grabs the toes of her tights in his mouth and pulls back. The tights stretch and stretch as Carla tries to wriggle free and gurgles with more and more laughter.

George is now almost at the other side of the room with the legs of the tights stretched to breaking point. He climbs on to the chair as Carla shrieks with laughter. George struggles to maintain his balance with the strain. A final wiggle from Carla and the tights come flying off as George crashes against a wall.

Horny as hell they bash again together, hands behind their backs, kissing like mad. George bites the arm of her T-shirt.

Carla, yer like a fucking onion, how many layers have you got on?

CARLA

Four. Scotland is a big fridge.

They kiss madly once again.

GEORGE

Fuck this, I'm using ma hands.

He spins her round so that she has her back to him. He whips off the four layers and immediately kisses her back.

GEORGE

Jesus!!

George jumps back in total horror at an enormous deep nobbly pink scar on Carla's back. He just can't believe his eyes. He comes to and realizes what he has done.

Oh Carla . . .

He moves towards her and tries to kiss her back. Carla spins round.

54

CARLA

NO!!

GEORGE

I want tae. I've got tae.

CARLA

Don't. Just hold me.

They fall back on to the bed. George hugs Carla for all he's worth.

GEORGE

Ah'm sorry . . . so sorry.

CARLA

I want to fight this . . . beat it, fight it, beat it, but I'm just so *rendído* . . . tired . . .

GEORGE

The letters . . .

CARLA

If only they had been . . .

GEORGE

What upset ye so much?

CARLA

Something terrible's happening . . . I don't know where to start . . . I don't have the words . . .

GEORGE

The letters.

CARLA

From my *compañero* . . . Antonio. He was hurt. Really hurt.

George hugs her.

GEORGE

It's OK.

CARLA

After this happened
                    (*indicating her back*)

I had to get away . . . out of Nicaragua . . . I couldn't sleep
. . . couldn't close my eyes . . . it was inside my head, around
and around inside my brain . . .

Easy . . . easy . . .

I ended up with a group of dancers and *musicos* travelling
Europe, raising funds . . . political work . . . talking about the
war, the US, the Contra, the war, the war, the killing, the war,
the war, the war . . . *a la gran puta*, day and night . . . day
talking, night screaming . . . at the end of the tour I had
nothing left, George . . . I couldn't go back, not one more
step . . . Final call for flight 714, final call for flight 714 . . . an
urgent call for Signora Carla Delgado . . . I spent a night in a
Heathrow toilet holding my ears . . . I stayed with some
Nicaraguans and Salvadoreans in London . . . but I was
losing my mind with guilt . . . more and more letters . . . I
never opened them . . . I got a ride up here. It was a good
place to hide. After that day on the mountain with you I
thought I could face it. You never asked anything of me. I
opened them.

What did they say?

Nothing . . . and everything.

What do you mean?

Songs. Simple songs. Some we wrote together . . . others we
just played . . . some we were working on . . .

He hugs her again.

What does *compañero* mean?

She hesitates. He squeezes her.

Friend. Friend of the soul . . .

GEORGE

Is that all?

CARLA

. . . and lover. Antonio was my lover.

GEORGE

What happened to him?

Carla cannot answer.

What is it?

CARLA

Promise not to ask.

George is stunned by her intensity.

Promise me!

George nods his head, almost frightened of her.

Swear it!

GEORGE
(*very quietly*)

OK Carla, I promise.

CARLA

On the life of your mother!

George hesitates.

Say it!

GEORGE

On the life of my mother.

CARLA

Now.

She bends down and kisses him. She bites George's tongue gently and extends it slowly from his mouth. She begins to bite it harder.

GEORGE

Ahhh.

Suddenly her body shudders with silent tears. She turns her back on him, but still cuddles in. George hesitates, then tries to kiss her back.

CARLA

Don't! Hold me.

George hugs her desperately.

A STREET: EARLY MORNING

George, huddled up, wanders along the street, drinking from a bottle of Irn Bru and eating a doughnut. He looks rough.

On the other side of the street a bunch of teenagers in school uniform wait for a bus. One of them recognizes George and gives Eileen an elbow. Eileen, like a Patriot missile, locks in on him. She sticks two fingers in her mouth and lets out a piercing whistle.

George recognizes it from the other side of the road.

EILEEN
(shouting)

Where hiv you been Romeo?

Her bus comes along the road. George sprints across the road to join her. He confronts Eileen and the other girls staring at him.

GEORGE
(mortally embarrassed)

Come here.

EILEEN

Whit?

GEORGE
(squirming and quietly mouthing under his breath)
It's private . . .

EILEEN
(right in the middle of the girls)
George . . . Ah canni hear yi . . .

58

GEORGE
(*spitting it out*)
It's private . . . Ah've goat tae speak tae yi . . .

The girls start whistling and shouting as the bus pulls up. They start climbing on.

EILEEN
Ah've exams next week . . .

GEORGE
Eileen!!

She can see he's serious. She takes one last forlorn look at the bus and waves it on. Her pals crowd round the window.

EILEEN
You're pushing yer luck.

The bus drives away.

A SMALL GREEN SPACE BY THE ROAD

George and Eileen are walking slowly side by side. Traffic intervenes. He is telling her the situation. She shakes her head in disbelief.

EILEEN
When did she ask ye?

GEORGE
Who?

EILEEN
Right, Ah'm warning ye George, Ah'm no in the mood.
Carla!

GEORGE
She disnae know yet.

EILEEN
Who says she's gonnie pack up and run off back home wi you
. . . a bit presumptuous!!

GEORGE
If Ah wuz her Ah'd run off wi me nae bother . . .

She looks at him in amazement.

EILEEN

George, there's a war on!! We're doing it in modern
studies . . .

GEORGE

Ah know there's a bit o' trouble.

EILEEN

A bit o' trouble!

GEORGE

Right. A war.

EILEEN

A war! Ye just don't know . . . dae ye?

GEORGE

More or less.

EILEEN

More or less!

GEORGE

Jesus Christ . . . will ye stop repeating what Ah say . . . Ah
can't stand that . . .

EILEEN

George . . . this is embarrassing. Right . . . There's the
Contras, OK? Contra means 'against' . . . right? Against what?
Against the Revolution. Against the Nicaraguan government.
Led by the Sandinistas. Who are the Sandinistas? Well, they
kicked out the dictator, Somoza, in 1979 . . . Now . . . this is
what's confusing Father Murphy . . .

GEORGE

What's confusin' Father Murphy?

EILEEN

The US is calling them Communists . . . *but* . . . there's three
priests in the government. They're going to screw the
Sandinistas. George.

GEORGE

The priests?

EILEEN

Naw! The US, ya dumpling! . . . and anyway, what if Carla takes off with this guy Antonio?

GEORGE

Ah've never been chucked in ma life.

EILEEN

Ah don't believe this. Yer serious.

GEORGE

Deadly serious.

Eileen has a right good look at him, trying to understand.

EILEEN

Hormones?

GEORGE

Ah love her.

EILEEN

What did you say?

George looks around him.

GEORGE

Ah said

(*still looking around*)

Ah love her.

EILEEN

You are serious.

She gives him a hug.

Mum will go bananas.

THE CAFÉ

Two Iberia air tickets are drawn from an envelope. Carla looks at them and her eyes fill up.

George is sitting with her in the same seats where they first met.

61

CARLA

Do you understand how . . . big this is?

George ponders this in his mind.

GEORGE

We canni bury this, Carla.

Long silence.

Am Ah right or am Ah wrong?

She nods her head.

Ah was scared ye would say that.

Pause.

Right . . . sort it out now . . . one way or the other.

CARLA

I don't even know where Antonio is.

GEORGE

We'll just have to find him.

Carla looks down.

GLASGOW AIRPORT

Their plane climbs steeply away from the ground.

FADE DOWN

INSIDE THE PLANE

FADE UP *on photographs in Carla's hands. The blinds are drawn and the photos are lit by the overhead reading lights. It could be night.*

CARLA

My mother . . . look . . . she got a new dress for the photo . . . Maruchi, Benjamin, Imelda . . . and Leonara . . . she doesn't smile because her teeth are missing . . .

She flicks over to a couple of photographs of herself singing and dancing with a group which bursts with energy. She looks supremely confident.

Our group.

She flicks to another, of a tough-looking mature foreigner holding a young child above his head in outstretched arms. Both he and the child are caught in a moment of spontaneous delight.

GEORGE

Who's that?

CARLA

Bradley.

GEORGE

Who's he?

It's as if Carla never heard.

Carla, who is he?

CARLA

Someone . . . just someone who helped me. We find him first, George.

GEORGE

Before your family? Why?

CARLA

He'll help us find Antonio.

This sends a cold shiver over George. He looks closely at the photograph of Bradley.

GEORGE

What's he do?

CARLA

Retired . . . Now he works for Witness for Peace. A US pressure group . . . against congressional funding for the Contra. They live in the war zones and record human rights abuse . . . we'll go there first.

GEORGE

Bradley. Is that his first name or surname?

CARLA
(*she shrugs her shoulders*)
He never talks about himself.

She flicks through a few more photographs of the same people. She turns over another photograph to reveal a handsome-looking young man with his arm round a beaming Carla. Then a close-up of the same man, smiling.

Carla quickly puts the photographs away. George knows better than to ask anything.

FADE.

View of Nicaragua from the plane window: morning light. The landscape is stunning: mountains, lakes and forests. Carla looks down. She turns to George. He is asleep.

ROBERTO HUEMBES BUS DEPOT. MANAGUA

Hundreds and hundreds of people mill around in a hectic tangle. Hordes queue for creaking buses that arrive jam-packed. Before the passengers can get off, the buses are once again swamped by teeming bodies.

Queues disintegrate into a struggling mêlée, everyone fighting for a place after hours of waiting. Children are thrown in windows, followed by agricultural produce, chickens, and yet more children.

A poor driver looks on stoically as his conductor struggles for calm. Another crammed bus crawls off leaning over to the right hand side, as so many hang on to the door, tilting it dangerously. The roof rack is a tangle of produce and younger men.

Carla and George struggle through the mêlée. They both have a rucksack and, between them, they carry a heavy bag. George is dying of thirst. Sweat runs down his face. Young market sellers weave in and out hawking their fruit drinks in plastic bags with loud melodic sounds.

MARKET SELLERS
Fresco fresco fresco . . . agua helada.

Carla stops George from buying one.

CARLA

You live in the toilet for a week!

She stops a seller who has a crate of Coke bottles. In a flash the young girl has emptied two bottles into plastic bags. Copying Carla, George bites the end of one bag and sucks it down in a oner before Carla can blink.

GEORGE
(*to the girl*)

Another one darlin'.

He just gets this to his mouth when there is a mad surge for the bus. He spills it all over himself.

George is not a happy man. His progress is handicapped by the heavy bag of shampoo and toiletries.

Carla fights her way on to the bus. George is separated from her and gets pushed to the side by the front door. The bus begins to pull out. He sees Carla desperately beckon him.

In a blind fit he throws on his rucksack, and the bag of shampoo. A couple of tubes fall out. George curses widely. Several kids run to pick up the tubes. He runs alongside the bus. Carla again shouts to him. The

Nicas love it. Beyond embarrassment he clings to the bus. Nicas start hauling him up as the conductor outside curses madly. The whole bus whistles, shouts, and laughs.

George is totally mortified, exhausted and panicked. Carla laughs out loud.

GEORGE
(*hanging on*)
Come back, Scratcher. All is forgiven!

Several women eye him up and joke with Carla on what a fine-looking fish she's caught. Every eye is upon him.

He gets himself a position on the front of the bus, squashed by the door, as the bus staggers out of the bus station.

ROADS IN MANAGUA

The bus turns a corner and belches black smoke as it gathers speed. George has a good view through the windscreen. He drinks in the newness. Buses swerve without warning to avoid potholes, old battered cars spewing fumes abound, there is the occasional horse and cart and old motorbike carrying families.

Posters are interspersed along the road; one encouraging breast-feeding, one that states, 'PEACE WITH DIGNITY' and another with a young Nicaraguan soldier leading a foreigner – at gunpoint – Hasenfus, a US mercenary who was shot down but parachuted from the plane to save himself. And graffiti: most notably the outline of Sandino's head and big sombrero.

The bus stops. George is pushed to the side in the rush of people getting on and off. The large bag splits open and shampoo and toothpaste fall out over some of the women. They pick them up with great interest and open them with no embarrassment to delight in the fresh smells.

CARLA
(*in Spanish*)

Presents!

Others stretch over to get a look. A man takes a deep sniff.

66

MAN
(in Spanish)
My wife would kill for this.

George hangs on as the bus goes on its way, past groups of soldiers and reservists, past market traders and past the revolutionary posters.

THE 'WITNESS FOR PEACE' BUILDING

A street corner: the bus drives in, stops, and George and Carla get down. George has the large bag, and throws a tube of shampoo to a Nica just inside the bus.

Carla walks up to the gate of an old building. A sign says in Spanish that it is the office of 'WITNESS FOR PEACE'.

She follows the path to the verandah, which wraps itself round the front of the building. On the far side, a group of people are having a meeting, grouped in wicker chairs around a low table.

Carla walks up to an American woman who is working on the verandah. George closes the gate and follows her. She has asked for Bradley.

WOMAN
You're in luck. He's down for a meeting. Wait there if you want.

She indicates some seats on the other side of the verandah. The meeting is partially in their sight. Carla looks for Bradley, her gaze settles on a tough and lean-looking fifty-six-year old, whose profile is turned away from them.

George puts down the heavy bag and sits or stands by Carla. They see a group of six or seven North American citizens, equally divided between both sexes. A gentle-speaking man in his mid-thirties chairs the meeting. All look very respectable, well organized and attentive with papers and pens.

Only Bradley looks a little out of place. He has folded and refolded a piece of paper into the shape of a concertina and rather disconcertingly begins to tear it into strips. He whistles slightly between his teeth. Though innocent enough, it distracts people's attention; something seethes underneath, and no one holds his eye when he looks up to a gazing face.

> **CARLA**
> *(quietly, so as not to disturb the meeting)*
> Their government murders us . . .

She nods to the circle.

> . . . their people risk their lives alongside us . . . some of the best people I've met in my life . . .
> *(shaking her head at the inconsistency)*
> Gringos!

They watch the meeting.

> **CHAIR**
> Item 12: Who'll take the diocesan delegation from Chicago? It's a group of 16, including the infamous Monsignor Ratzinger.

> **VOICES**
> Ohhh . . .

> **CHAIR**
> . . . right-hand man to the Archbishop.

> **VOICE**
> God himself . . .

God bless him. A law professor, teachers, and mostly church workers.

Their own transport?

Yip.

Spanish?

Own translator.

Two hands go up.

Right, Ed and Francis.

A feature writer from the Mississippi Steam Boat Express, circulation 22,000 . . .

Two hands go up.

Monica and Roberto.

And, wait for this . . . Edwin Seeth of *The Times*.

Hissing sounds.

Wants to visit 'war-savaged border areas and interview amputees' and is accompanied by an award-winning photo journalist, Paul McCormick.

Silence from everyone. Bradley continues to tear the paper. Tension. He shakes his head.

George, listening intently, catches Carla's eye. He mouths silently: 'Is that him?' She nods.

Perhaps someone else volunteers. The chair lets it pass.

Right, last item. This month's Human Rights reports . . .

They all start passing their typed-up reports to Bradley. They pile up before him.

Bradley . . .

Bradley picks up a big report at random.

BRADLEY

This is Witness for Peace . . . not *War and Peace*.

He turns over the report and looks at the name.

It took me three days to get down here for this meeting; I don't have time to collate this sentimental trash . . .

He opens the report.

'My eyes filled with tears as I examined the burnt-out remnants of their humble home . . . in my mind's eye I thought back to the conversations I had with Enrique's dead wife . . .'

Jesus . . . thank you, Mary Lou Tolstoy Baker . . .

She looks totally crushed.

VOICES
(shocked and intermingled)

For God's sake, Bradley . . . Sick and tired . . . That's totally unfair . . . it's her first report . . . don't take this personally Mary . . . Chair . . .

George once again catches Carla's eye.

BRADLEY

I want date, time, location, fatalities, civilians or otherwise, and how many Contras. *Punto*!! Final!! Life's too short. Get some literary critic to collate this dross, or your biographer if you're that important.

He picks up all the reports, leaves the group and makes for a clearing in the garden where he starts loading supplies on to an old battered jeep.

Carla and George move to follow him. Carla hesitates, and watches him load the supplies with an almost demonic energy. George nudges her. She walks towards him, but doesn't say anything. He starts ever so slightly. Intelligent eyes take everything in immediately.

Well . . . will you hug me?

He hesitates. Drops the bag in his hand and gives her a strong but tender hug.

How are you?

Older.

He continues to load the jeep.

You?

I'm OK.

He stops and stares right into her.

He starts loading the jeep again.

I don't know where he is, Carla.

This stops Carla in her tracks. Awkward silence. Bradley notices George.

CARLA

I need a drink. Bradley, this is George.

George moves forward and offers Bradley his hand. Bradley dutifully shakes it.

GEORGE

How're ye doing?

CARLA

Let's go.

She leads the way across the road and just round the corner to a small bar looking on to the street.

A BAR

A small army vehicle bumps past a bar which faces a junction of three roads. Bradley, Carla and George walk up to a shop which has tables and stools outside. More graffiti: on one wall the distinctive face and sombrero of Sandino; George and Bradley sit as Carla asks for three beers.

GEORGE

So who's the guy with the big hat?

No reply. George is not sure if Bradley heard him, but is deterred from repeating the question.

CARLA

Right, tell me, who have you seen . . .

BRADLEY

I keep myself to myself.

CARLA

Luis? . . .

Bradley shakes his head.

Oyanka? . . .

Bradley shakes his head

Amarillis? . . . Daniel?

CENTER: **BRADLEY**

No. No . . .

CENTER: **CARLA**

Rafael?

CENTER: **BRADLEY**

Rafael sends me illegible scrawls now and again on bits of paper this size . . .

He demonstrates a tiny little square.

Carla smiles at the thought of him.

CENTER: **CARLA**
CENTER: (*to George*)

He teaches literacy.

CENTER: **BRADLEY**

He's on the move . . .

Carla's face falls.

Last I heard he was being worked to death by Norma out of Esteli and trying to escape her . . .

Carla laughs out loud at the thought of her.

Speak to Norma . . . if she can spare thirty seconds.

CENTER: **CARLA**
CENTER: (*to George*)

She's tough!

Carla looks relieved. She picks up Bradley's map for George's benefit and points to the north of the country. She circles 'Esteli'.

We'll find her here . . .

She points to the north of the country by the border with Honduras. She indicates a tiny settlement called San Cristobal.

This is where my family live now . . . forced out of Esteli . . .

CENTER: **GEORGE**

How come?

CENTER: 73

The Somozistas were after my brothers . . . Here's the main US base.

Where's that?

Bradley watches him carefully.

Just across the border in Honduras . . . they have a free hand and do what they like . . .

She points to a tiny settlement right on the border, but still close to San Cristobal.

> (*to Bradley*)
Are you still here?

He nods. Carla circles a settlement called 'Esperanza' and shows it to George.

This is where Bradley carries out his heroics . . . the big white man . . . and where he practises the art of conversation, of course . . .

A smile crosses his eyes for the first time.

. . . and right here . . .
> (*indicating a point close to Esperanza*)
the biggest Contra camp . . .

> (*looking up from the map to Bradley*)
Tricky.

Suddenly Bradley leans across and grips George's arm. Bradley holds up his own hand to him in demonstration. He bunches the fingers and thumb of his right hand together so that there is a tiny hole at the top. With vibrating fingers he makes the hole bigger and smaller by turn.

> (*to George*)
Do that. Do it!

He's so extreme George must copy.

Your sphincter!! The muscles around your orifice.

CARLA

Stop, Bradley.

BRADLEY
(*looking straight into his face and now speaking so quietly*)
When was the last time you were so scared, so terrified.

CARLA

Stop it!

BRADLEY
(*his fingers vibrate like crazy*)
So paralysed, that you were taken over by your ass-hole . . .

CARLA

Shut up, Bradley!

BRADLEY
. . . thus the reflexive verb, to shit oneself. Tricky, very tricky.

George is humiliated.

CARLA

Bradley! . . . have you seen Antonio?

BRADLEY
(*shaking his head*)
Could be dead for all I know.

GEORGE
(*jumping up*)
You're a callous bastard!

BRADLEY
(*getting up and gathering his things*)
And you're an ignoramus. What the fuck are you doing here?

CARLA

For God's sake! Bradley!

He goes to Carla. Holds her and kisses her unexpectedly.

BRADLEY

I'll be going north tomorrow evening, if you're around.

He strides off with great energy. George looks destroyed. Carla gently touches his arm.

CARLA

He's difficult . . .

GEORGE

He's a fucking nutter.

CARLA

We'll find Norma and Rafael . . . they'll know where he is . . .

GEORGE

Carla . . .

He hesitates.

CARLA

What is it?

GEORGE

I've got to ask you this . . .

76

She tenses up.

. . . Could he have died?

Carla nods.

I'm sorry.

She leans across, kisses his cheek and lays her head on his shoulder. He puts his hand up round her hair.

CARLA

Are you OK?

GEORGE

I don't know.

TOP OF AN OLD BUS: AFTERNOON

George bounces nine inches in the air from the roof-top of an old packed bus as it hits a teeth-crunching pothole. He curses to himself and rubs his arse.

An old campesino *beside Carla grins at him openly and nods at him every now and again. George forces a polite nod back.*

The campesino *and his two companions yap to Carla. George can't take his eyes off her as her hair blows in the wind and as she gives the old man such care and attention. They talk twenty to the dozen and they all burst out laughing. The* campesino *points to his brand-new wellies. Others join in. With great care, he pulls a piece of paper from his bag. Carla takes it carefully. Her face shines. The old man grins.*

They pass rice fields peppered with beautiful birds with long white necks, and ramshackle buses, just as packed. They slow down at a bridge guarded by several young soldiers with AK 47 machine-guns. More nods from the old campesino *who monitors his curiosity.*

A huge IFA truck crammed with young soldiers, many with red and black Sandinista colours on their hats or around their necks, thunder past. Several on top of the bus raise their arms in mutual salute to the soldiers, including a grinning Carla. The old campesino *nods at George. George nods back.*

Through a little town. Chaos as the bus is surrounded by those getting on, those getting off, and a swarm of young girls and women selling frescos *and* chicharon. *George leans over as Carla hangs on to his legs. Money changes hands and he emerges with three plastic bags of purple drink, one for each of them, and one for the* campesino *who nods gratefully.*

CAMPESINO
¿Que siembran en tu pais?

George looks helplessly at Carla, and smiles at the campesino *in embarrassment.*

CARLA
What do you grow?

George looks really confused.

GEORGE
What dae Ah grow?

CAMPESINO
¿Hay arroz?

He lifts up a bag of rice and shows him.

George shakes his head.

¿Hay maiz?

He looks about for another bag. Another listener hands him corn on the cob.

George shakes his head.

¿Hay frijoles?

He shows him some beans.

George shakes his head in guilt.

The old campesino *shakes his head too in great sympathy.*

Que pais mas maldito!!

CARLA
(*translating, with a shrug*)
What a God-forsaken country!

GEORGE
(*mumbling to himself*)
Cheeky old bastard.

George fumbles inside his rucksack.

(*Carla translates*)
Ah'll show you something that took ten years to grow . . .
inside a bottle!

He triumphantly holds up what he has been looking for.

Whisky.

Carla starts laughing. The campesino *and others on the bus recognize
the magic word and join in. George unscrews the top and hands it to
him.*

*He stares at the bottle. George indicates that he should take a swig. He
sniffs it, enjoys playing to the audience and then for the first time in his
life tries the golden juice. The entire bus top is transfixed. He wipes a
rough hand across his mouth and savours the taste. He takes another
long swig. They all await his verdict.*

CAMPESINO
(*in Spanish*)
What a fucking wonderful country!

*There are cheers from the top of the bus. An older woman beside the
campesino sniffs the drink and George indicates that she should try as
well. Carla is really enjoying the laugh.*

CARLA
(*in Spanish, to the hesitant woman*)
Go on . . . it's good for your liver . . . lovely and sweet . . .

*She takes a swig and spits it out immediately. More shouts from the bus
top. Carla bursts out laughing and they both catch each other's eye.*

79

CAMPESINO
(*in Spanish, annoyed*)
It's a God-damned sacrilege . . . that's ten years' work you just spat out, woman!

He grabs the bottle from her, as the bus takes off in a plume of smoke.

The old campesino *digs out his piece of paper once again and hands it to Carla.*

Go on tell him . . . tell him . . . go on . . .

CARLA
(*to George*)
Two hundred *manzanas* of land were transferred into the name of their co-operative . . .

The campesino *continues his nodding and grinning.*

CAMPESINO
(*in Spanish*)
Have you told him? . . . Eh. Have you told him? . . . I want to tell everybody!! Especially '*cheles*' . . .

Many on top of the bus begin to laugh. Carla touches his arm delicately.

CARLA
He says that ninety families have what once belonged to one man . . .

CAMPESINO
(*waving his drink around*)
Revolución!

The Nicas are really beginning to enjoy him.

The campesino's *dander is really up; he swings his drink, then points to the paper in Carla's hands.*

(*in Spanish*)
The land . . . Ours! The coffee . . . Ours! The gold mines in Limon . . . Ours!! The port in Corinto . . . Ours! The banks . . . Ours! The Revolution . . . Ours! The guns . . . Ours!

On the last 'Ours' his over-enthusiastic gesticulation sends the bottle of whisky flying over the side.

ESTELI

The bus station. A square teeming with activity: street traders, kids and passengers. A large Sandino looks down from a wall. Carla and George dismount and are immediately surrounded.

The bus reverses then drives out, belching black fumes. Carla hoists her rucksack on her back, then suddenly turns in the direction of the disappearing bus.

CARLA
The bag . . . we left the bag . . . my presents.

She races to where she can see it disappearing down the street. George joins her. He tries to look sympathetic but can't hide his delight.

Carla is quietly furious. He pokes her but she doesn't respond.

GEORGE
It wuznie the crown jewels Carla . . . a few tubes o'shampoo.

CARLA
(*spinning round*)
Have you any idea what a few simple things mean in the middle of the war?

She storms off. George is left to catch up.

They walk across the square, past a large mural of FSLN (the Sandinista Front) leaders; past a building battered by the war, and down the main street.

A loudspeaker van passes, with an announcement about the war and a militant song.

Carla strides ahead. George ducks and dives past the stalls that litter the pavement and the boys who want to clean his shoes.

AMNLAE BUILDING

They reach the offices of AMNLAE, *the women's organization. On a wall is Sandino's outline and some graffiti. George catches up.*

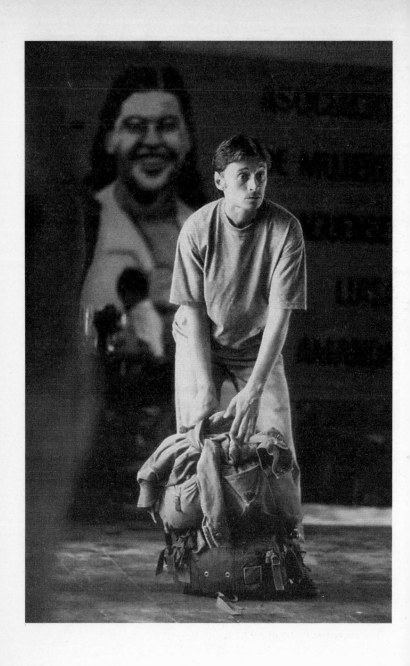

CARLA

For your information the 'guy' in the 'big hat' is Sandino.
Wait here.

George is left standing as Carla disappears into the building.

*An older black woman is one of a group who are unloading clothes and
sewing-machines from a truck. She has heard Carla's remark and goes
over to George. She takes him by the shoulder and they face Sandino.
Her English is spoken with a rich Atlantic Coast accent.*

WOMAN

Sandino . . . a freedom fighter . . . betrayed and assassinated
in 1934 by one Anastacio Somoza . . . a second-hand car
salesman installed by the gringos . . . and then we had two
more of the sons of bitches till the Sandinistas kicked their ass
in '79. Cost us 50,000 lives . . . and my *compañero*.

George stares up at her in amazement.

GEORGE

Where are you from?

WOMAN

Nicaragua.

He's confused.

The Atlantic Coast.

GEORGE

Yir English is dead good.

Her face lights up with amusement.

WOMAN

Thank you. It is my first language . . . another one of your
colonies.

GEORGE

Might as well take the shagging blame for that as well!

She laughs heartily. George looks at the graffiti.

'*El pasado no volverá jamas.*'

WOMAN

'The past will never return.' But I wouldn't bet on it.

Carla returns.

GEORGE

I'm really sorry about your presents.

It disarms her.

Is Norma here?

She nods at him.

CARLA

Still in a meeting.

Carla enters again. George turns round and catches sight of the woman watching him with a wonderful twinkle in her eye.

AMNLAE BUILDING: INTERIOR

As George and Carla walk in they are passed by a mixture of different internationalistas.

They stand together in the central part of the building which opens out into a garden at one end. The place is bursting with activity.

Carla points to a woman who is doing her best to sort out a variety of problems.

CARLA

There she is . . .

She leaves George with her bags and runs over. Norma is overwhelmed to see her. Many hugs and exclamations of joy. George waits.

In another corner there is a bunch of young women in full military uniform, with AK 47s stacked behind them, playing cards in the shade.

One of the girls clocks him, and he nods to her sheepishly. They joke at his growing shyness. He tries to tidy up his dishevelled appearance, but it simply provokes more comment. Lobster-faced after hours in the sun on top of the bus, he's obviously dying for a drink. One of the girls holds up her army water container. He takes his courage in his hands and shyly walks over and takes it from her. He can't get the top off. They try to hide their laughs into their hands.

> GEORGE
> (*quietly, to the container*)
> Open up ya bastard . . . what a brass neck . . .

The girl jumps up and twists it open in a flash. He holds up his arm, indicates his biceps, and then points to hers. One of them makes an obviously dirty crack about checking out his muscles. He gulps down the water like a man in the desert.

Muchos muchos thankyous!

Carla and Norma approach him. George looks at Carla to make sure she is OK.

Norma warmly takes his hand.

> NORMA
> (*in hesitant English*)
> Do you like our place?

> GEORGE
> The United Nations.

Norma laughs warmly.

> NORMA
> Many little friends . . . but one big enemy.

Norma catches another preoccupied look from George.

> (*to George*)
> I saw Antonio six months ago, just before he left hospital . . .
> I've tried to make contact . . . but it's difficult . . .

> CARLA
> (*sudden frustration*)
> Rafael must know where he is!

Norma instinctively takes Carla's arm, and George notices a flash of deep concern in her face.

> NORMA
> Rafael is close by . . . You can visit him tomorrow.

A friend shyly (but very excited to see her) beckons Carla. She crosses over.

Norma watches Carla for a second and then she stares at George, sizing him up. The moment passes and she's back again to the practical.

So what can you do for us?

GEORGE
What do you mean?

NORMA
What can you do for us?

George is taken aback by the question. Norma holds his eye.

There is an almighty scream. A woman with a telephone shouts loudly for Norma. Norma sprints towards her. The woman with the phone looks pale-faced. Women surround her. George can see her speak and there is a surging burst of emotion. Some cry, others shout. More women rush from the adjoining rooms.

The women soldiers run from the building. Other women stand silently. Some hug each other in tears.

George looks for Carla but can't see her. He's shocked and totally frustrated. He grabs a foreign-looking woman.

GEORGE
What's happened?

She's very upset, and speaks to him in Italian. He turns away and asks someone else.

GEORGE
What's going on?

WOMAN
They ambushed a bus as it hit a mine . . . seventeen dead, and dozens injured . . .

GEORGE
Carla! . . . Carla!

He runs madly about, looking for her. Norma is already calling for silence and issuing very practical instructions (about where to get a list of names, supporting family, emergency fuel, and the urgency of blood donors).

He catches sight of Carla who is down on her hunkers, leaning against the wall. She has her hands to her eyes and her body is racked with silent tears. George kneels in front of her and cuddles her among the legs, movement, chaos, and Norma's voice above it all.

HOSPITAL ROOM: EVENING

George and Carla sit side by side with their backs against a wall. It is very quiet and almost peaceful. There are four others in the room with them. They all give blood.

Carla has her eyes closed. George is almost mesmerized by the gradual bulging of the plastic bag beside him filling with his blood.

> CARLA
> (*very quietly, and still with her eyes closed*)
> I want you to go home, George.

George doesn't answer but takes her hand. Their fingers entwine.

> GEORGE
> Do you mean that?

> CARLA
> I mean it . . . but I'm scared.

> GEORGE
> Me too . . .

> CARLA
> I want you to think about it . . . and be honest with me.

> GEORGE
> I'm not leaving you, Carla.

> CARLA
> There's so much to tell you . . .

A nurse begins to take the needle from George's arm. Someone is already ready to take his place.

87

GEORGE
We'll see this through together.

THE HOSPEDAJE JUAREZ: EVENING

George and Carla walk towards the hospedaje *(hostel) on the street corner. As Carla enters, George's eye is caught by a bunch of kids playing baseball. A young disabled ex-soldier in an old wheelchair is in the middle of the bedlam. He pitches the baseball (a stone wrapped up in a sock) and does his best to referee.*

George follows Carla inside. She is negotiating with a woman for a room. An old man in a rocking chair watches, a twinkle in his eye. A deal is done and George follows Carla and the woman.

They pass through a tight little passage which has rooms on one side and a charming but overgrown garden on the other. A couple of parrots, perched by the passageway, let out noisy squawks.

Carla moves into a room.

GEORGE
(*quietly, to the parrot*)
Your Uncle George has had a difficult day. Keep me awake tonight . . .

It makes a snap at his fingers.

. . . and I'll have you and your pal scrambled for breakfast
. . . right.

There is a noise of squeaky springs from inside. George enters the little room, drops his bags on the floor and looks around. Not bad. Then he sits down beside Carla. The bed sinks way down in the middle and again the sound of really noisy springs.

Suddenly the lights shut out. Loud whistles and groans from outside. George jumps with fright.

What the hell . . .?

CARLA
Relax . . .

GEORGE

My bloody nerves!!

CARLA

It's the old generator . . . they warned me . . . no spare parts
with the US embargo . . .

There is the noise of creaking springs as George sinks on to the bed.

GEORGE

Never mind the generator, how about getting some fucking
decent mattresses into this country . . .

The parrots start squawking.

. . . Oh man . . . I need a hug!

Noise of the mattress as Carla lies down beside him.

HOSPEDAJE JUAREZ: LATER

A little light seeps in through the door.

*Strange night noises that leave George tense. Buzzing of mosquitoes.
Carla tosses and turns in her bed half sobbing, half moaning in Spanish:
she sweats profusely.*

Fractured flashes of songs and dance of Carla and compañeros *in
performance before an enthusiastic audience.*

*It jumps from a group piece to Carla dancing solo, pushing herself to the
limit as Antonio plays guitar.*

As it ends, a parting Carla catches his eye for a special moment.

*Carla's voice calls out: 'Antonio!! Antonio . . . corre corre!!'
In her sleep she tosses her head violently. She mutters 'corre . . .
corre . . .'*

*The intensity of her fear frightens George, who is up on one elbow,
watching her.*

*He puts out his hand to her, but stops in case his touch terrifies her. He
doesn't know what the hell to do. Gradually her wails turn to a
whimper.*

He hears noises like guns in the distance though he can't be sure.

HOSPEDAJE JUAREZ: EARLY MORNING

The house and rooftops of the town in the early light: a rumbling sound of trucks crawling through the streets. Light filters through the shutters in the room in the hospedaje. *George opens them and looks out. Carla joins him. An enormous East European IFFA army truck turns the corner beside them and trundles past. Followed by another, then another and another.*

Dozens of young teenagers in army uniform, armed to the teeth, cram the back of each vehicle. Many wear the distinctive red and black colours of the Sandinistas around their caps. They look no older than the boys who were playing baseball.

Mothers, daughters, lovers and sisters wave goodbye.

GEORGE

They're just boys.

Beside one of the trucks, one mother, highly distressed, cries, shouts and gesticulates to other mothers and a soldier in charge. She grips on to the shoulder of her upset son and refuses to let go. Her hurt is so genuine it touches them all.

What's wrong with her?

CARLA

She says the Sandinistas have no right to take her son . . . she
disagrees with Military Service . . . and she says he will die . . .

*The boy kisses his mother, forces her hands from him, and then runs to
the back of the truck where he gets a hand up from his pals. The mother
sinks to her knees as other mothers surround her. The truck takes off,
and the young boy stares back, tears streaking his face, at his hysterical
mother waving her hands in his direction. A pal throws an arm round
his shoulder in support.*

RAFAEL'S SCHOOL

*George and Carla are riding down a dirt road in the back of a small
pick-up. Others are crammed in with them. They cross a small bridge
where women are scrubbing clothes on the rocks while skinny naked kids
play in the water.*

*The truck pulls up outside a simple school building. Carla and George
get out and the truck drives off. Carla is apprehensive.*

*They get closer. The teacher says something in the distance. There is a
peal of laughter. Now she knows.*

CARLA

It's Rafael.

*The class is full of adults some of whom are very old; a mixture of men
and women, all of whom look typically* campesino.

Carla's eyes shine as she sees Rafael guide the stiff fingers of an old
campesino *woman who writes her name with chalk on the blackboard.*

*There is a long list of names on the board, some fairly neat, others
sloping and irregular like those of a child.*

The old woman finishes, shyly delighted with herself.

George sees Carla is deeply moved.

The last of the campesinos *moves to the board. He is a tall wiry man
with strong gnarled fingers. With studied intensity he begins to write his
name as Rafael gives him encouragement.*

CAMPESINO
(*in Spanish*)
Son of a bitch . . . how come I've got such a long name.

More laughter. Carla unintentionally lets out a gentle giggle. Rafael turns immediately and catches sight of her. He can hardly believe his eyes. He is desperate to go and hug her, but he is committed to helping his elderly student finish his name.

RAFAEL
Bueno . . . bueno . . .

The campesino *scrunches up his eyes to admire his work. His name,* PURIFICACION, *stretches out beyond all the others at a strange angle. Rafael is now desperate to greet Carla.*

CAMPESINO
Momento . . .

He approaches the board once again. Rafael's face drops. He methodically dots the three 'i's.

RAFAEL
Muy bueno compañero . . .

He approaches the board once more. Rafael holds his breath. He proudly stamps a full-stop.

(*in Spanish*)
Right . . . that's us till Thursday . . . well done.

All the campesinos *file out.*

Carla stares at Rafael across the empty classroom. They move towards each other as George stays where he is watching them both hug each other. They are very emotional. They speak in Spanish.

Where have you been . . . I've been worried sick . . .

CARLA
It's a long long story . . .

RAFAEL
Oh . . . it's so good to see you . . . let me look at you.

(*urgently*)
My family . . . are they OK?

RAFAEL
Your mother's been going crazy . . .

She cringes slightly.

(*noticing her guilt*)
. . . but she'll be so glad to see you . . . you've got to get up
there straight away . . .

CARLA
Are they OK?

RAFAEL
They're fine . . . they're still in San Cristobal.

CARLA
Thank God . . . thank God . . . and . . . Antonio?

RAFAEL
(*trying to ignore her*)
You've gone all skinny . . . a bag o bones . . . too much
European health-food? . . .

CARLA
Antonio!?

George flinches at his name. Rafael hesitates.

RAFAEL
Just leave it, Carla . . .

CARLA
Don't fuck me about, Rafael!

RAFAEL
Ask Bradley. He'll know more than anyone.

CARLA
I've just seen Bradley! He knows nothing!

RAFAEL
Neither do I.

She looks at him and knows he's lying. She grabs his shirt.

CARLA
(*desperately*)

Is he alive?

Rafael grabs her to him and hugs her to his chest.

RAFAEL

Oh Jesus . . . yes . . . he's alive . . .

CARLA

Have you seen him?

RAFAEL
(*very emotional*)

I've seen him. About four months ago . . .

CARLA

How is he?

RAFAEL

Not doing well . . .

CARLA

Where is he?

RAFAEL

I honestly don't know, Carla . . . he said he didn't want to see any of us again and just disappeared . . . but he's been in contact with your mother . . . that's all I know, I swear . . . go back to your family . . .

He holds her for a little while.

From George's point of view: he feels torn, worried for her, but determined to give them privacy. He slides to his hunkers against the wall. Carla turns round to George.

CARLA

George.

She beckons him over. George squirms with embarrassment and shakes his head.

Come here . . .

Naw . . .

George!

GEORGE

You two have a wee talk . . . I'll go for a walk . . .

Rafael is sensitive to the situation. He takes Carla by the shoulder and they both walk over to George.

Rafael takes him warmly by the hand.

RAFAEL
(*in halting English*)
My name is Rafael . . . any friend of . . .
(*pointing to Carla*)
. . . she . . . is a big friend of me.
(*pointing to himself*)

George smiles at his openness and takes his hand.

GEORGE

Big amigo you too . . .

He makes Carla chuckle in spite of herself.

Are you OK?

She takes then both by the waist and starts walking with them.

CARLA

I need a big drink . . .

As they walk off they both put their arms round her too.

RAFAEL
(*in Spanish*)
It's so good to see you, you little bandit . . . have you written any more songs?

She shakes her head. He suddenly picks her up and starts running down the hill with her screaming over his shoulder.

We'll have to fatten you up!

George and Carla sit by the roadway, waiting for a lift or a bus, with a few others and a handful of kids. Carla is downcast.

He desperately wants to cheer her up as her spirit falls. He snuggles up beside her and bites her ear. She shrugs him off.

GEORGE

Did Ah ever tell yi what a wonderful pair of *orejas* yi hiv . . .

She can't hide a rising gurgle . . . he touches her earlobes.

She grabs his finger and bites it. Two watching little girls giggle. George examines his finger.

Dedo.

Then his own hair.

Pelo.

A wee boy joins the group. Carla points to her eye. George struggles to remember.

(*to the girls*)

Don't tell me.

Carla writes 'ojo' with a stick on the sandy ground.

(*with exasperation and totally mispronouncing it*)

Ohjoe!!

The kids burst out laughing.

BOY

Ojo!!

Suddenly George turns on him, and as if pulling a gun from his holster, sticks his finger to the pit of his stomach, and in totally fluent Spanish:

GEORGE

Manos arriba – esto es un robo!![1]

The wee boy immediately sticks his hands up in a semi-panic. Carla is absolutely pissing herself, as are all the adults who heard.

1 Hands up – this is a hold-up!

George blows his index finger as if it were a gun.

   Magnificent Seven. Yul Brynner!

An old man beside them has been listening.

OLD MAN
   Butch Cassidy . . . Paul Newman!

A bus approaches in the distance.

GEORGE
What does '*corre corre*' mean?

CARLA
(*slightly puzzled*)
   Run, run.

The bus teems with bodies.

GEORGE
   I don't know if Ah can face this.

The bus pulls up beside them. George and Carla stand by the front as people fight to get on.

There is an almighty bang and sizzling noise from the engine; billowing smoke. The bus driver jumps out cursing like mad. His conductor joins him.

They throw open the front bonnet and jump back as more putrid fumes surge upwards. The conductor fans the engine with an old cloth, clearing the fumes to reveal a clapped-out engine. George and Carla move closer, as the driver tentatively inches forward with an old rag. He wipes at the grease and dirt to clear his view.

Suddenly a jet of steam hisses from a worn hosepipe into the driver's face. He cries out in pain.

Carla, behind George, explodes in a berserk fit; shrieking, moaning and howling, her body in bizarre vibration.

Kids start crying, adults cower back, while others hesitate. George jumps forward to hold her, but she attacks him in a fury, clawing at his face with her nails. George can't contain her frenzy.

97

A jeep screeches to a halt in the middle of the bedlam.

> **BRADLEY**
> Carla! Carla!

She recognizes his voice immediately. She stops and then collapses.

Stupefied, George watches on as Bradley picks her up, laying her down gently on the back of his jeep. Two older women hitch-hikers cradle her head without emotion.

George, in one swift movement picks up their rucksacks, throws them in, and jumps into the seat beside Bradley.

Still stunned, George turns around to look at Carla. She is out cold. Bradley switches on the ignition. George takes Carla's limp hand.

> **GEORGE**
> You'll be OK, Carla . . . OK.

This infuriates Bradley.

> **BRADLEY**
> You know something? In my time I've done business with pimps, mercenaries, molesters . . . Mother Teresa . . . evangelists and cock-sucking politicians . . . but there's only one set of dick-heads I can't tolerate . . . *optimists.*

George is stunned.

> Have you any idea what you've been putting that girl through?

> **GEORGE**
> What are yi talking about?

> **BRADLEY**
> Go fuck yourself.

He accelerates away.

A HOSTEL: NIGHT

On the balcony, George gently pushes Carla in a hammock. She tosses and turns in uneasy turmoil.

In a shy and self-conscious voice, close-up and very quietly in her ear,

George sings the first verse of an old traditional Scots lullaby.

GEORGE

Hush hush, time to be sleeping.
Hush hush, dreams come a creeping,
Dreams of peace and of freedom,
So hush, bonnie bairnie, my ain child . . .
Hush hush, time to be sleeping
Hush hush . . .

She bursts into an inaudible babble then sits bolt upright. George is unsure whether she is about to have another fit and freezes himself. He watches her intently. Her eyes are wide.

FLASHBACK: AT FIRST WITHOUT SOUND, THEN WITH DISTORTED SOUND: OUT OF PERSPECTIVE

An open-backed lorry charges through a rough track. Young brigadistas *of a cultural brigade blast out a song with gusto. A good-looking guy beside Carla plays a guitar. Antonio and Carla hold each other's eye as their voices soar above those of their friends. Rafael is beside them.*

The lorry accelerates down hill towards a shallow pool. As the water sprays to either side the brigadistas *shout in delight.*

A rake of bullets sprays the students, turning white shirts to red. An RPG grenade smashes through the windscreen, blowing the cabin to smithereens. The lorry rolls back into the river, and then flicks over like a toy. The side of the truck traps a wounded student in the water.

Antonio and Carla are thrown clear with several others. They duck, crouch and slither around as the contras move in. Total chaos ensues as the few students with guns try to return fire. Rafael fires twice then manages to escape.

Antonio grabs Carla's arm and runs alongside the narrow river. She stumbles and falls. Her shirt is covered in blood. Brief glimpse of several Contras giving chase. They charge into the bushes. Antonio sees they're catching up. He throws Carla into long grass and runs as decoy.

He bolts into other Contra and is surrounded.

Deep panting sounds. Focus on Carla traumatized in the bushes. She can

99

*hear groans. Several Contras are very close by. Between the long grass she
can see their backs; they carry US M19s, grenade launchers, wear US
uniforms and shell pouches which have clear US stamps on them.*

*Antonio screams. Carla shivers in terror. She takes a quick look between
the blades of grass. One of the Contras has a rope and approaches
Antonio.*

*Focus on Carla as a terrible deep-throated gurgling sound engulfs her.
She looks up again. Only a quick flash. Antonio, hands behind his
back, is dragged around by the rope. His feet struggle desperately to keep
up, but her view is blocked by the reeds.*

Close-up of his feet kicking up dust, desperately trying not to fall.

*Desperate moans, sounds of blows, and Spanish imperatives. Carla
curls up in the foetal position, gripping her ears. She whispers to herself.*

CARLA

Antonio, *amor . . . corre corre.*

Sheets of paper and music float down the river.

BALCONY: DAWN

Carla lies in the hammock, eyes wide. After a moment she looks over the side and sees George, fast asleep beside her in a chair. She watches him with tenderness for a few seconds and then gets up quietly from the hammock. She walks along the balcony to a door, opens it and slips inside.

HOSTEL: BRADLEY'S ROOM

Carla approaches Bradley's bed. He wakes with a start. Carla sits on the edge of his bed.

> CARLA
> Why did you lie about Antonio?

Bradley rubs his eyes.

> How is he?

> BRADLEY
> As stubborn as an old mule.

Carla laughs.

> Been attacked three times in the last month. Refuses to move. Stupid dicks think it's some kinda symbol . . . They killed his brother . . .

> CARLA
> José?

> BRADLEY
> No, he joined the Contras. The youngest . . . Pedro.

Carla bows her head.

> Why did you come back?

> CARLA
> George.

Bradley shakes his head.

> No . . . he's right . . .

> BRADLEY
> Does he know?

Carla shakes her head.

> CARLA

But he's still right . . . he saved me, Bradley . . . I love
him . . .

Bradley stretches out and takes her hand.

> BRADLEY

Antonio?

> CARLA

I can't bear him, but can't forget him.

> BRADLEY

It's too much, Carla.

> CARLA

I must stop running, Bradley . . . and so must you . . . Where
is he?

Pause.

> BRADLEY

He lives with me.

> CARLA

I'm coming with you.

> BRADLEY

Over my dead body. I'm bringing you home.

*Carla sits by him in silence. The sound of her voice fades in. Singing
strongly. The song is* 'Cambia Toda Cambia' (*Everything Changes*).

COUNTRY ROADS

*Bradley drives at great speed on narrow dirt tracks in the hills. Carla
sits by him, singing. George, in the back along with the compulsory
entourage of those hitching a lift, bounces uncomfortably at every
pothole.*

*A young kid with a bandaged arm touches George's white skin. She
feels the hairs on his arm and smiles up at him.*

George starts a 'thumb' game with her. George holds up his thumb and just as she's about to grab it, it disappears into his fingers again. She becomes obsessed trying to get his thumb, and eventually triumphs, grabbing it tightly with her good arm.

The sound of distant firing. Carla stops singing, her eyes scanning the hills. Perfect countryside for guerrilla warfare. Bradley notices her strain.

They head down a slope into a narrow river. The water sprays to each side. Carla grips her rucksack so tightly. Bradley leans across and massages her hand. She loosens off.

The remnants of a bridge poke above the water. Campesinos, *weighed down with produce, wade across to a waiting mini-bus that cannot cross. George notices a young man carrying a nervous old woman in his arms. She holds a white hanky over her eyes.*

They come around a steep corner and turn to face the remains of a recently burnt-out bus. Two women are making a shrine for those who died in the fire.

An older woman in the back of the jeep taps Bradley on the shoulder. He stops, giving her an understanding gesture.

George moves to Carla, who turns her head from the bus quite obviously not wanting to look at it. She picks up the map and in reply to George's puzzled look she points once again to the circled point to which they are travelling.

Bradley turns off the ignition of the jeep. The silence seems overpowering. The woman blesses herself by the bus and begins to pray. Others from the jeep join her.

Bradley nervously looks up at the hills. George notices.

Suddenly they hear the distant sound of artillery. An army jeep screeches around the corner followed by an IFA truck full of young soldiers. Every face is deadly serious as they all contemplate combat. Eyes scan the countryside. Every gun ready. No posturing. Fear communicates itself.

SOLDIER
(*in Spanish*)

What happened?

103

(*in Spanish*)

Nothing.

SOLDIER
(*in Spanish*)

Got to move. They're close.

The soldier's eye lingers over George.

. . . and 'The White One?'

BRADLEY

With me.

The jeep screeches off. Bradley pumps the horn. One of the young passengers notices something.

NICA

A la gran puta!! Bradley . . .!

Bradley sprints to join a young Nica at the back of the jeep. After a quick examination, he kicks the bumper in frustration. It is loose, and after kicking it, he has to make sure that it'll stay on. He's twice as frustrated.

George runs around to look at the problem.

A steady trickle of diesel runs from the corner of the tank. An old solder has worn away. The Nica holds his finger to it, but it still dribbles out. Bradley runs to look at the gauge to see how much is left. He looks at his watch, and then at the hills.

He kicks the jeep again.

BRADLEY

Shit!

GEORGE

Have you any soap?

BRADLEY

Soap?

GEORGE

Soap.

Carla rummages about in her rucksack and hands George her soap.

For once Bradley is unsure of himself. George hesitates; enjoys his discomfort.

George rubs the bar of soap on the corner of the diesel tank; an ingenious temporary repair.

Bradley stares at the tank, then George.

> Start her up.

He does so. George examines it once again.

> It'll do.

He jumps up on to the back of the jeep and sheepishly acknowledges the smiling faces. He hands Carla back her soap.

> See what a University education does fir yi.

Bradley has a very private grin to himself.

SAN CRISTOBAL

The jeep drives into the village. Carla's eyes drink in the familiarity; George the newness. They pass children filing from the school, a few with chairs on their heads.

A couple of women recognize Carla and wave in spontaneous delight. Carla returns the wave with growing excitement. George watches her in wonder, moved for her. Some kids now recognize her. More waves.

Bradley stops in a little square opposite a simple building now used as the Health Centre. There is a sizeable queue, mostly women with children. A nurse dressed in immaculate white calls in the next patient. Bradley lifts the kid with the bandaged arm from the jeep.

A huddle of bodies, mostly women and children, now run towards Carla. George recognizes her mother half running, half walking, half laughing, half crying. Carla looks up. Her mother stops, almost paralysed by the moment. They run towards each other, hugging and weeping. After a good look at each other, Carla's mother bends down and picks up a toddler and puts him in her arms. Carla hugs him tightly.

René . . . René . . .

She is engulfed with kids, shouting and pulling at her. Her mother wipes her tears and tries to tidy her straggly hair, before taking the child from her again.

George notices Bradley watching intently from the jeep; a trace of a smile. He takes off suddenly.

Carla waves enthusiastically at George. She laughs through her tears at his embarrassment, runs towards him, takes him warmly, so warmly, by the arm and brings him through the chaos towards her mother.

GEORGE

Yo me llam . . .
> *(getting mixed up)*

. . . se llamo . . .
> *(more mixed up)*

. . . fuck it . . . ma name's George, Mrs Delgado . . .

He gives her a spontaneous big bear hug.

Mucho gusto!¹

He sounds so raw and honest Carla bursts out crying. All three hug in the midst of the mêlée.

CARLA'S HOME

George sits at a simple wooden table. He downs the last two spoonfuls of soup and grimaces. Carla savours each spoonful.

George stares at the simple surroundings; the thin plywood dividing walls only three quarters up to the roof; the hard-packed dirt floor; an almost identical Sacred Heart to that in his own home, the Virgin Mary, a poster of Sandino, Lenin, and a black and white framed photo of a young man with a pencil moustache. There is also a prominent portrait of Archbishop Oscar Romero of El Salvador.

Carla's mother enters to clear away the plates. George lifts up his T-shirt, pats his stomach and gives her the thumbs up. She smiles shyly and pats him on the shoulder.

1 A great pleasure.

She disappears again into a backyard.

A pleasant rhythmic tapping sound begins.

Carla cocks her head and smiles.

CARLA

My mother.

The noise stops and then a similar one begins again. Slightly different beat.

Leonara.

George looks puzzled.

Again the next tapping rhythm.

My mother.

Carla's face shines. George is touched to see her steeped in the familiarity of her surroundings.

Home!

More tapping.

Thank you George Lennox.

GEORGE

What for?

CARLA

Just thanks.

George still looks puzzled. Carla indicates that George should follow. From the door they can see Carla's mother and Leonara making a huge pile of tortillas. Each in turn takes a neat handful from a pile of maize paste and, in a jiff, each with their own unique rhythm has tapped out and flattened a tortilla and thrown it on top of a hot-plate over an open fire.

George is fascinated by their speed of hand.

They smile at George. George smiles at them.

LEONARA
(*in Spanish to George*)

Do you dance?

George looks lost. Leonara gives a sway of her hips and holds up her hands. George, embarrassed, shakes his head.

(*in Spanish to Carla's Mum*)

He's got a cute little ass!

VILLAGE: NIGHT

A sizeable crowd mills round the entrance of Carla's house. A party to welcome Carla home is in full swing.

George stands in one corner surveying outrageous merry-making. He sways gently gripping on to a tumbler of rum in each hand.

The ambience sweeps over him; George winks at the Sacred Heart, holds up his tumbler, and drinks a toast. From the other tumbler he toasts Karl Marx.

The music is provided by the world's worst mariachi band, totally absorbed in their own art form. They wear shabby but immaculately clean and perfectly ironed mariachi suits; only their footwear gives them away. One wears ridiculous white boots and another short working wellies.

George focuses on Carla, marvelling at her beauty as she gesticulates and laughs to her friends and relatives who surround her.

He takes another swig of rum and offers it to a young campesino *who stands beside him, clapping George's back in approval.*

He feels chuffed and proud as Carla looks his way as she talks to a huddle of her cousins and aunts and mother who all, without the slightest embarrassment, eye George up and down with x-ray vision. There is a peal of laughter at an old aunt's raw joke. George toasts them with his tumbler, and the laughter bursts out again. Tears of mirth stream down Carla's face.

The young campesino *of eighteen or so smiles approvingly at George with a certain unabashed innocence.*

GEORGE
(*to campesino*)

Ah don't know how to say this . . . but she gets me right
there.

He taps his heart.

The campesino *taps his T-shirt. They take another drink.*

CAMPESINO
(*in Spanish*)

Swap you shirts.

GEORGE

Ah just really fancy . . . her. Know what Ah mean?

He taps his heart again.

But there's a big . . .
(*lost for words and tapping his forehead*)
. . . riddle . . . in her heid . . . but no here!
(*tapping his heart*)
What can Ah do but be myself. Eh?

CAMPESINO
(*in Spanish*)

Yours for mine!

*The music swells up and through the dancing bodies George's eyes follow
Carla around the room. Another swig. The* campesino *raps George's
chest and then points to his own.*

GEORGE

You fancy yer chances too . . . eh?

George laughs and claps him on the shoulder.

Well, tough!!

Campesino *now pinches his T-shirt from his chest with some
exasperation. He points at George's T-shirt with 'City of Glasgow'
printed on it. He pulls off his shirt and hands it to George.*

Nae problem, wee man!

With great enthusiasm they change shirts. George has a shirt with

Sandino, faded and holed, and the young campesino *shows off his distinctive new shirt. Carla's mother and aunts laugh at the exchange.*

Sweating bodies dance around the dirt floor. Old grandmothers to young kids sway in perfect rhythm to a salsa.

Outside the door an IFA lorry crunches to a halt. Dozens of young soldiers appear outside the house. Whooping and yelling. Many are engulfed by friends and relatives. Several make their way in and look straight away for Carla.

More hugs and mad embraces. Sheer mirth and celebration.

George watches on with fascination. It sets the campesino *off too.*

CAMPESINO
(in Spanish, so George doesn't understand)
It would break your heart this war. So much hurt.
Sometimes . . .

He hands George his tumbler of rum.

GEORGE
Cheers . . .

CAMPESINO
(in Spanish)
. . . and I'm only saying this to you because it'll go no further
. . . sometimes I find a quiet corner all by myself and I cry my
eyes out . . . other times

He gets the tumbler back.

. . . I just get so angry . . .

He shows George the tattoo on his arm. His name is 'Harry'. George can hardly believe it.

GEORGE
Hey . . . Harry!

They laugh together. The mariachi band strikes up a Palo de Mayo – an extremely erotic Caribbean dance, rhythmic and pelvic. A young soldier dances with Carla as all the relatives and soldiers crowd

110

*around them. Whoops and shouts as the dance progresses. George can
feel his insecurity rise as he sees Carla enjoy herself so much on her
own terms.*

*Suddenly Carla pulls George in, in place of a disappointed soldier who
was chancing his arm just a bit too much. George, well gone, gives a
very passable attempt cheered on even more enthusiastically by the circle
around them.*

BALCONY: NIGHT

*Carla and George cuddle in a single hammock. They watch the
stragglers leave the fiesta. Suppressing their laughter, they see two old
drunks, one standing beside his mule, shake hands with his friend. They
shake hands again and again which reminds George of home.*

*At last one of them tries to mount his mule which he finds near
impossible. He gives up and they go back to shaking hands.*

George and Carla cuddle in passionately.

> GEORGE

Carla, I don't want to risk this . . . *for anything!*

This alone is enough to pass a cold shadow over them.

Did you find out anything about . . .

> CARLA
> *(putting a hand to his lips)*

We'll talk tomorrow.

She rolls on top of him and kisses him. She gives him the eye.

> GEORGE

In a hammock?!

She nods.

Is there danger money?

VILLAGE

*Irregular buzz of crickets and cockerels in the distance. A dog begins to
bark. The hammock sways ever so gently. Carla rests her head on*

George's chest; both fast asleep. The first red of dawn appears in the sky. A baby cries way off in the distance.

The rope of the hammock creaks gently as they move involuntarily in their sleep. Carla murmurs gently, her hand feels George's shoulder, and then she settles down again. Creaking of the rope.

Sudden crescendo of noise as the roof of the building explodes in a ball of flames. George and Carla are catapulted away from the inferno that was the house.

Cacophony of explosions, yells, and heavy machine-gun fire.

Close-up of Carla and George lying on the ground. Carla lies motionless, in the foetal position, with her back to George.

George comes to and sees Carla.

GEORGE

Carla. Carla. Jesus, Carla.

He rolls her over. Her face is expressionless and her eyes wide open. George stands up to lift her.

The campesino *with whom George changed shirts, screams at George.*

NICA
(in Spanish)

Down! Down! Run! Run!

George stares dumbfounded at the chaos around him. The Nica runs at George and in a perfectly timed rugby tackle knocks him flat. He grabs one of Carla's arms. He has an AK 47 machine-gun in the other. George takes Carla's other arm as the Nica screams at him. They crawl to a trench and drop over.

The Nica pushes George and Carla to the bottom and then disappears over the top again.

GEORGE

Sweet Jesus, what is this?

George cradles Carla's head in his trembling arms. Her face lights up with the intermittent explosions.

A body lands on George. He screams in a panic. He can't see in the

112

dark and throws the body off him.

In a huge flash he can see the same campesino. *George catches a glimpse of the T-shirt. Blood pumps from a wound in his chest. 'City' is clear but 'Glasgow' is covered by a huge red patch.*

The body moans and begins to shake violently in the dark. This seems to bring Carla to life. She picks up the dying man and the two silhouettes huddle close together as George looks on dumbfounded.

VILLAGE: DAY

George and Carla stand in the street: a scene of absolute destruction.

The simple school and Health Centre are now smoking ruins. A nurse pokes among the debris, trying to save some medical supplies which haven't been totally burnt. Several women are comforting children and cooking outside. Carla speaks to them.

George helps to salvage things from the school: books that smoulder, chairs that are burnt. He sees children among the ruins, pigs rooting among the burned-down store for corn and men carrying wounded.

He sees Bradley, who is carrying a body on a makeshift stretcher. The body is dressed differently, but is still very young. George notices a US stamp on his uniform. Bradley takes the pulse on his neck.

> BRADLEY
> (*to Carla*)
> Have you seen the doctor? The Frenchman?

> CARLA
> He's dead.

> BRADLEY
> We might get some press coverage.

He takes his pulse once again.

> Too late anyway.

Bradley looks into the Contra's pockets. He pulls out distinctive photographs of the terrain from on high, and a map, momentarily flicks his eyes over them, and sticks them in his pocket.

George, shocked at Bradley's control and overcome by the trauma, stares at him.

Rich man's money. Poor man's blood.

George turns away. He sees Carla disappearing into the wreck of the building that was her home. He follows her.

CARLA'S HOME

George knocks on the door gently and enters. It's the same room where the dancing took place. Carla sits at an old wooden table with a young infant on her knee. Carla's mother taps George gently on the back, and wanders out again. His eyes look red.

> GEORGE
> (*very gently*)
I've been thinking, Carla . . .

> CARLA
George, this is my son.

George takes her hand gently and squeezes it.

> GEORGE
Come home with me, Carla. Now! Bring the baby, I don't care.

She puts her head down.

George desperately waits for an answer.

> GEORGE
Antonio's kid?

Carla nods.

Do you know where he is?

> CARLA
I do now. He stays with Bradley up in Esperanza.

George looks even more confused.

> GEORGE
Carla, can ye tell me? What is it with you two?

Carla looks overcome again.

Are yi together? Do ye love him or what?

Carla cannot answer him.

OK Carla. OK.

Long pause.

This is all beyond me. I'm going back. I'll wait one day for ye . . . at that wee *hospedaje* . . . in Esteli. After that I'm going home. It's done ma head in.

He looks down at his blood-stained T-shirt.

All this killing . . . pure madness . . . fucking chaos.

George stands up to leave.

CARLA

It's *not* chaos.

George gives her a look of complete loss. He kisses her cheek and for a few horrible moments he puts a few things into his rucksack. The grating sound of the zipper.

GEORGE
(indicating the child)

I wish the baby was mine.

George walks out, deeply upset, with the rucksack over his shoulder. He passes Bradley at the door on the way in without saying anything and disappears. Bradley stares at Carla, clearly moved, as tears stream down her face.

VILLAGE STREET

George walks through the village to where an old jalopy of a medium-sized bus is waiting. Some of those with minor wounds are going for treatment.

George makes for the open door of the bus. A noise from the back: a big driver makes a tutting sound – the Nica equivalent of 'Hey, you'. The driver waves a finger at George telling him not to get on.

Bradley calls him from across the street.

BRADLEY

I'm going to buy you a drink . . .

He doesn't stop for an answer and is already by him, walking in the direction of the bar.

GEORGE

I want nuthin from you . . .

BRADLEY

You're going to need a drink.

GEORGE

I need fuck all from a twisted bastard like you . . . Why did you lie about Antonio?

BRADLEY

(*over his shoulder as he disappears into the bar*)

Hurry up.

GEORGE

Fucking prick . . .

George follows in a furious temper.

THE BAR

Simple bar. Bradley walks in and orders. George shouts at him from the door.

GEORGE

You've been lying to us from the very beginning . . .

Bradley emerges from the bar with two glasses and a bottle, sits down at a table on the verandah.

More secrets stuffed up yer arse than 007 . . . Why can't you just tell me the truth . . . nice and simple.

Bradley pours him a drink.

BRADLEY

OK. Nice and simple. They caught Antonio in an ambush. Tied his hands behind his back and sliced out his tongue.

116

GEORGE
(*almost gagging on his drink*)

Oh Jesus!

BRADLEY

As he lay choking they smashed his spinal column with the butt of their rifles.

GEORGE

What the fuck is going on here . . . Jesus Christ! Oh fuck, fuck . . . Animals . . . fucking animals . . .

BRADLEY

Those animals are wearing grey suits . . . the nine to five brigade going back to their families . . . look at the map . . . every detail planned with precision.

He points to the map on the table taken from the Contra.

US satellite photos . . . taken by the US government. Look at the targets: schools, hospitals, bridges . . . I know because I was one of them . . . I had my hand on that knife . . . I sliced out his tongue . . . sweet irony . . . in the name of 'democracy'.

GEORGE

What is all this? . . .

BRADLEY

It's money, always money . . . It's not just about Nicaragua . . . for every dollar the US invests in Latin America, it sends back three . . . do you see . . .

GEORGE

Naw, Ah don 't see . . .

BRADLEY

. . . in a continent with over 300 million people, most of them poor, hungry, illiterate . . . in a land of plenty . . . half of them starve . . .

GEORGE

. . . but . . .

. . . their wealth sucked North . . . and here . . . the People have said *no*! They've said *no*! Broken with history . . . dreamt and fought for change . . . dared to put their people *first* . . . Feed them, heal them, teach them to read and write . . . believe me, that's a threat . . .

GEORGE

What threat?

BRADLEY

. . . of a good example . . . What happens if 300 million say *no*! Brazil says *no*! Peru says *no*! Mexico says *no*! What happens when a people take control of their own resources for themselves? . . . That's the threat they must exterminate . . . that's why all this suffering is so carefully planned . . .

George studies him, struggling to take it in.

You should have seen those two together . . . heard them sing . . . simple beauty . . . She's never seen him since that day . . . I never finished my tale . . . you see, we old experts in Low Intensity War have a nice antiseptic turn of phrase: 'violence for propagandistic effects' . . . disturbs the mind . . . and it takes three to look after a cripple, a corpse just rots, manures the land . . . as he lay there, Antonio, choking and paralysed, they poured acid all over his face . . . and you know who saw all this . . . don't you?

GEORGE

Naw . . . Naw . . . Ah've got to see her . . .

He sprints towards the door.

STREET AND CARLA'S HOUSE

George runs to Carla's house in a frenzied panic. He reaches it and bursts in.

GEORGE

Carla!! Carla!! Ah didnae know!

There is no sign of her. Carla's mother appears frightened at one entrance holding Carla's son.

> MOTHER
> (*in Spanish*)
> She's already gone to Esperanza.

She keeps repeating it until George recognizes the name of the co-operative.

> GEORGE
> (*distraught, to the mother*)
> Ah didnae know! I swear to Christ Ah didnae know!

Carla's mother pulls an envelope from a deep pocket and hands it to George. He looks down on his name and his address in Scotland. He tears it open.

> CARLA
> (*voice-over*)
> Dearest George,
> Forgive me. So close. So far. I cannot face this nightmare. I am in no fit state to love you, my son, or Antonio. My life is poisoned. Day and night. Bradley will explain. He is a good man who shares my torment. Be kind to him. I have caused you great hurt. You have been so gentle. So long.
> Carla.

George is totally overcome. He catches Carla's mother's eye for a second and touches her arm. He sprints out.

THE STREET

George runs like he's never run before. Total and absolute exertion. He grips the letter in his hand. Exhausted, he arrives at the bar.

> GEORGE
> Bradley!! Bradley!!

Bradley bursts from the door.

> Where's your jeep . . .?

BRADLEY

What . . .?

GEORGE

Come on!! Fuck you . . . Hurry up!

He hands Bradley Carla's note.

She's gonnie do herself in . . .

Bradley takes the note. George sees the jeep and starts running for it.

BRADLEY

There's no diesel . . .

George swings round desperately to look at him. He looks up at the bus still in the same spot. The driver is leaning against the rear talking to a woman. The engine is running. George jumps into the driver's seat and takes off. The driver falls over, curses and starts running pathetically after the bus as George charges on.

Bradley rushes out in front of the bus and forces George into an emergency stop. Bradley jumps on.

GEORGE

She'll kill herself. She tried twice in Scotland . . . Ah've got to get to her . . .

BRADLEY

Think! There's Contras everywhere.

GEORGE

Get the fuck out then.

Bradley jumps off. He picks up two AK 47s standing up beside the wall and jumps on again. Two milicianos *sitting on the wall close by run towards them.*

BRADLEY

Move it.

GEORGE

Why you?

BRADLEY

Why not?

George rams the bus into gear and accelerates, just as the bus driver catches up again. With absolute confidence he slips through the gears, charging towards a group of soldiers at the edge of town who wave him down. They scatter at the last moment, cursing, shouting and throwing up their hands in exasperation.

SOLDIER
Suerte loco!

The bus swerves around a bend and is swallowed up in steep hills.

George catches Bradley's eye. He gives him the 'sphincter' sign with vibrating bunched fingers.

BRADLEY
Me too!

THE ROAD TO ESPERANZA

The bus bounces along the rough track. George handles it with great skill but still struggles to keep control. Bradley, with obvious knowledge, prepares both AK 47s.

GEORGE
Thought yi were now a pacifist?

BRADLEY
I resign.

He is thrown about as the bus recoils and ricochets off each pothole.

He runs up the side of the bus, randomly smashing a few windows. He strikes out the back window too with the butt of his rifle and crouches down.

Further down the track:

They come to a sudden fork.

BRADLEY
Left!! Left!!

George just makes it. An old campesino *woman tries to wave them down and points in agitated fashion ahead of them. George accelerates.*

GEORGE

(*shouting above the crashing motion of the bus and labouring engine*).
How far?

BRADLEY

Keep driving!

The engine begins to smoke with the abuse. It labours as they slow to the brow of the hill. George curses viciously. Over the hill and dangerous acceleration. The brakes hardly work.

A hail of bullets smashes the windscreen and chassis.

A la verga!! Cabrones!!

Bradley punches out the shattered windscreen so George can see.

GEORGE

Get down, for Christ's sake.

Bradley jumps to a window and lets out a continuous burst of machine-gun fire.

ESPERANZA: DUSK

The bus swings round a bend. Lights in a tiny settlement twinkle 500 yards from them. George flashes his lights.

The bus limps into the heavily defended co-op. Bradley and George jump out of the burning wreck.

Suddenly the bus is surrounded by young men blasting their guns off. Apart from one or two most are in their teens.

George stares at them. They stare at him. Some examine the bullet holes in the side of the bus.

Several have surrounded Bradley and joke with him for being suicidal. They banter away.

Bradley beckons over a young soldier he knows well.

BRADLEY

José . . .

He doesn't have to ask.

JOSÉ
(*in Spanish*)

She's in Anne Maria's house. Wanted to be alone. She looks really bad.

BRADLEY
(*to George*)

She's in there.

(*pointing where Carla is*)

My house, last on the left. I live there with Antonio.

George runs towards the shack. Yards from it he stops and slows down. He approaches tentatively.

Bradley and the soldiers watch him from the distance.

George pushes open the door. Carla is crouched on the floor.

He kneels in front of her and holds her tear-stained face. He pushes her untidy hair behind her ears and rubs his forehead to hers.

CARLA

Take me home.

George kisses her tenderly.

GEORGE

You are home.

He takes his wallet from his hip pocket. He pulls out two carefully folded pieces of paper. Red stained paper. George unfolds them and gives them to Carla.

Her hands tremble as she looks down on the words, recognizing Antonio's letter immediately.

CARLA

All he ever asked was that I touch him once. Just once . . .
The first time we ever met was to rehearse this song . . .

George slowly stands up and takes her arms. She shakes her head. George nods.

He takes her by the hand and leads her to the door.

Carla freezes. She can see the silhouettes and faces at every door.

George takes her by the hand and they begin the long walk towards the last simple wooden house. He is aware of faces and movement on either side. The sound of their feet. He strides towards Bradley seated on the step of his house watching them approach.

The fingers of George's hands intertwine with Carla's. In the other she grips the sheets of paper.

As they get closer they can hear the gentle strumming of a guitar. Bradley's house is darker than the others, lit by a flickering candle.

George and Carla stop in front of the house beside Bradley who is sitting on the step.

GEORGE

It's up to you now.

Carla hesitates and then enters. George sits beside Bradley. The guitar stops. Bradley and George sit motionless. The crickets seem deafening and George thinks his heart will burst. It feels like an age.

The guitar starts a beautiful gentle melody ('Guerrero de amor'). After a few moments Carla's voice tentatively, gently, trying to control itself, begins to accompany him.

Her voice breaks. The guitar stops for a second. He begins again. Carla joins in, barely in control.

Stronger. The door swings half open. George and Bradley look over their shoulders. In a dark corner Carla and Antonio sit opposite each other; the shadow of his wheel-chair. The music grows stronger. Carla's voice begins to soar. Some neighbours stop at the steps. Antonio accompanies her perfectly on the guitar.

The chorus builds up gently and powerfully, Antonio strumming like mad as Carla's voice holds every note perfectly. On it goes. Beautiful, beautiful harmony.

Through the door Bradley and George can see Carla and Antonio very close. The song ends. She leans across and takes his hidden cheeks in her hand and their foreheads touch.

Silence. Silence.

George looks up at Bradley. He has the fingers of one hand pinching his eyes. Tears flow down his cheeks. George punches him on the chest. They both lower their heads.

A ROADSIDE SETTLEMENT

The usual chaos as a bus gets ready to leave. The driver's assistant shouts 'Managua, Managua'. Bradley's jeep pulls up by a huge mural of Sandino. George pulls his rucksack from the back. The driver's assistant takes it from him.

> ASSISTANT
> *(in Spanish)*
> Do you want to go on top?

George nods.

> BRADLEY
> Did you get that?

> GEORGE
> Perfecta-fucking-mente, hermano.

The assistant hurls the rucksack to a pair of hands on top.

> BRADLEY
> She asked me to give you this.

George opens the battered envelope. He takes out the song on red notepaper. Silence between them for a moment. George turns to Bradley after putting it in his breast pocket.

> GEORGE
> What did you do?

> BRADLEY
> *(pause)*
> CIA . . . Tegnicigalpa, 81–84, Honduras. You?

> GEORGE
> Bus-driver.
> *(pause, then mysteriously)*
> Double-decker, number 72 and 76. Glasgow.

(*pause*)
All this . . . *stuff* . . . hard to believe . . . eh?

BRADLEY

Hard to believe, George.

George catches his eye, aware that Bradley has used his name for the first time.

The bus assistant starts shouting to George to get on the bus. Bradley and George look at each other awkwardly, then shake hands.

The bus moves off. George runs and jumps on to the ladder by the back door. He turns to Bradley and simultaneously they give each other the sphincter sign.

He laughs out loud for the first time.

The bus accelerates and hits a big pot-hole. It disappears in a cloud of dirty fumes.

EPILOGUE

ON THE 11 AUGUST 1985 THE CONTRAS CAPTURED TWENTY
PEOPLE FROM ACHUAPA. THE GROUP WERE DIVIDED IN TWO.
SEVEN WERE KIDNAPPED AND THIRTEEN WERE TORTURED BY
POURING ACID OVER THEIR FACES. SELFIDA CASTRO RECOGNIZED
HER SONS BY THEIR HANDS.

IN 1987 ANTONIO RIOS WITNESSED THE CONTRAS TORTURE A
MAN BY 'POKING A HOLE THROUGH HIS TONGUE, PLACING A
ROPE THROUGH THE HOLE AND DRAGGING THE MAN AROUND
THE CAMPSITE BY THE ROPE'.

ON THE 27 JUNE 1985 THE INTERNATIONAL COURT OF JUSTICE,
THE JUDICIAL BRANCH OF THE UNITED NATIONS, FOUND THE US
GOVERNMENT GUILTY OF NINE DIFFERENT VIOLATIONS OF
INTERNATIONAL LAW AGAINST NICARAGUA.

ON THE SAME DAY THE US CONGRESS APPROVED AN ADDITIONAL
100 MILLION DOLLARS TO THE CONTRAS.

IN A SWORN AFFIDAVIT BEFORE THE COURT EDGAR CHAMORRO,
EX-INFORMATION OFFICER FOR THE CONTRAS, TESTIFIED, 'THE
ATROCITIES I HEARD ABOUT WERE NOT ISOLATED INCIDENTS,
BUT REFLECTED A CONSISTENT PATTERN OF BEHAVIOUR BY OUR
TROOPS. THERE WERE UNIT COMMANDERS WHO OPENLY
BRAGGED ABOUT THEIR MURDERS AND MUTILATIONS.' THE
ENTIRE OPERATION WAS 'CREATED BY THE CIA: IT WAS
SUPPLIED, EQUIPPED, ARMED AND TRAINED BY THE CIA: AND
ITS ACTIVITIES – BOTH POLITICAL AND MILITARY – WERE
DIRECTED AND CONTROLLED BY THE CIA.'

APPENDIX 1

The American General Smedley D. Butler wrote:

'I spent thirty-three years and four months in active service as a member of our country's most agile military force – the Marine Corps.

'I served in all commissioned ranks from a second lieutenant to major general . . . and during that period I spent most of my time being a high-class muscle-man for Big Business, for Wall Street and for the bankers . . .

Thus I helped make Mexico safe for American oil interests in 1914 . . .

I helped make Haiti and Cuba a decent place for the National City Bank to collect revenues . . .

I helped purify Nicaragua for the International banking house of Brown Brothers in 1909–1912 . . .

I brought light to the Dominican Republic for American sugar interests in 1916 . . .

I helped make Honduras 'right' for American fruit companies in 1903 . . .

In short I was a racketeer for capitalism . . .'

APPENDIX 2

1926   US Marines invade and occupy Nicaragua.

1926–31 Guerrilla army under General Sandino fights US occupation.

1934   Nationalist guerrilla leader Sandino assassinated by Somoza, head of US-trained National Guard.

1936   Somoza seizes Presidency, and with US support establishes a dictatorship by the Somoza family lasting forty-three years.

1961   Sandinista Front (FSLN) founded, named in honour of Sandino.

1979   FSLN leads popular insurrection, Somoza flees, FSLN takes power – with a revolutionary programme of land reform, free health care and education, the mass literacy crusade, etc.

       CIA begins to organize the remnants of Somoza's defeated National Guard into a counter-revolutionary force, the Contra. 'Low-Intensity Warfare' begins; lasting 11 years, costing 30,000 lives.

1980   Reagan replaces Carter in USA, Contra war stepped up, with units operating from both Honduras and Costa Rica, receiving support and training from CIA and US military.

       Contra forces include ex-National Guard, kidnapped forced recruits, mercenaries from various countries, and Nicaraguans opposed to the Sandinistas. They are financed by a mixture of official and covert US Administration funds plus private anti-communist crusaders and CIA takings from drugs and arms deals (see 'Irangate' etc.).

1984   First clean, free elections in Nicaragua: FSLN wins with 67 per cent of the vote (turn-out of the electorate: 82 per cent).

1986   World Court finds US guilty of illegal military intervention in Nicaragua. (Nicaragua claims $17 billion in war reparations, but later drops the case after US pressure, following Violeta Chamorro's victory.)

1990   Elections: FSLN emerges as biggest single party with 42 per cent of the vote, but is defeated by the US-backed coalition UNO, made up of fifteen parties (ranging from demobilized Contra groups to the Communist Party!).

Violeta Chamorro becomes President.